The Social Organization of Schools

New Conceptualizations
of the Learning Process

The Social Organization of Schools

New Conceptualizations of the Learning Process

Edited by

Maureen T. Hallinan

University of Notre Dame
Notre Dame, Indiana

Plenum Press • New York and London

Library of Congress Cataloging in Publication Data

The Social organization of schools.

Papers presented at a conference held at the University of Notre Dame, May 13–14, 1985.
Includes bibliographies and index.
1. School management and organization—United States. 2. Ability grouping in education. 3. Education—United States—Curricula. 4. Educational equalization—United States. 5. Educational sociology—United States. I. Hallinan, Maureen T.
LB2805.S687   1987   370.19   86-30577
ISBN 0-306-42428-2

© 1987 Plenum Press, New York
A Division of Plenum Publishing Corporation
233 Spring Street, New York, N.Y. 10013

Printed in the United States of America

To my parents
with love and appreciation

Contributors

Rebecca Barr, National College of Education, Evanston, Illinois

Charles E. Bidwell, Department of Education, University of Chicago, Chicago, Illinois

James S. Coleman, Department of Sociology, University of Chicago, Chicago, Illinois

Robert L. Crain, Teachers College, Columbia University, New York, New York

Robert Dreeben, Department of Education, University of Chicago, Chicago, Illinois

Maureen T. Hallinan, Department of Sociology, University of Notre Dame, Notre Dame, Indiana

Nancy Karweit, Center for Research on Eelementary and Middle Schools, Johns Hopkins University, Baltimore, Maryland

James M. McPartland, Center for Research on Elementary and Middle Schools, Johns Hopkins University, Baltimore, Maryland

John W. Meyer, Department of Sociology, Stanford University, Stanford, California

Aage B. Sørenson, Department of Sociology, Harvard University, Cambridge, Massachusetts

Preface

This volume addresses key issues in the sociology of education concerning how schools are organized for instruction and what processes link school organization and instruction to educational achievement. The content of the chapters represents a shift in focus from traditional and even recent themes in sociology of education, including the study of school effects and of classroom processes, to a concern with the social organization of schools and its consequences for student outcomes. Rather than reviewing or evaluating existing research, the chapters present new and developing conceptualizations of the schooling process and provide theoretical models to guide future empirical work on schools.

A unique feature of this book is its heavy emphasis on theory. Each chapter presents a theoretical model or argument concerning an issue of central importance in sociology of education. The empirical analyses and simulations that are included are often more for illustrative purposes than for rigorous hypothesis testing, and some chapters have no data analysis at all. The major strength of the volume, therefore, lies in the new conceptualizations and reconceptualizations it provides of fundamental processes relating school organization to student learning. Theoretical work such as this is exactly what is needed in an area that has traditionally been, for the most part, empirical and atheoretical.

Another important feature of this volume is the various approaches it presents to the study of school organization.

Although the nine chapters in the book overlap considerably in object of study, they represent a variety of approaches and perspectives, from macrosociological to microsociological analyses and from institutional to individual foci. This plurality of perspectives makes the chapters complementary and represents a significant contribution to the study of schooling, which, typically, has been characterized by a disjointedness of emphasis and effort.

The first chapter is an introduction to the volume and an overview of its contents. The next five chapters are concerned primarily with the organization of the curriculum and of students for instruction. In Chapter 2, Dreeben and Barr present the curriculum as an organizational feature of a school and examine the coverage of instructional material as it relates to distributional properties of instructional groups, the characteristics of curriculum materials, and the availability and use of classroom time. In Chapter 3, Hallinan extends a previously formulated model of learning to portray the processes that link within-class ability grouping to student achievement.

In Chapter 4, Karweit analyzes issues of educational excellence as they are associated with methods of grouping students for instruction and illustrates her model with simulated data. Chapter 5, by Sørensen, looks at the organizational differentiation of students in schools and in particular their assignment to academic and nonacademic tracks and the consequences thereof for educational opportunities. He supports his arguments with an analysis of the first two waves of the *High School and Beyond* data.

Chapter 6, by McPartland and Crain, focuses on the tensions that exist between efforts to improve the effectiveness of schools and efforts to provide equal educational opportunities for all students. The organization of students for instruction, according to the authors, plays a critical role in the attainment of these two goals.

The last three chapters of the volume address questions related to the effects of school organization on learning as mediated by school, community, and societal relationships. In

Chapter 7, Meyer examines the implications of the institution-alization of education for learning and for the organization of instruction. Chapter 8, by Coleman, analyzes the relationship between the social structure of a school and the network structure of the community for which the school was established. Relying on ethnographic data on three schools from dramatically different communities, he develops a theory of organizational and network effects on school outcomes. In Chapter 9, Bidwell examines how the recruitment of students and teachers to schools is related to the social organization of schools and how this interrelationship influences the school's function as an agent of norm transmission and as a setting for the development of the capacity for moral judgment.

The primary audience for this book is scholars and researchers in the fields of sociology, psychology, and education. It will be of particular interest to those who study issues in sociology of education, organizations, and the curriculum. The book should also appeal to educational practitioners who wish to draw upon a theoretical framework to inform policy decisions about such issues as the assignment of students to groups or tracks for instruction, the pace and content of instruction, curricular choices, norm transmission, and community ties.

This volume grew out of a conference, "Conceptualizations of School Organization and Schooling Processes," that was held at the University of Notre Dame, May 13–14, 1985. I am deeply grateful to the University of Notre Dame for funding this conference. The intellectual and physical environment of the university made the conference not only possible but also successful. Special appreciation is expressed to Timothy O'Meara, Provost, and Michael Loux, Dean of the College of Arts and Letters, for encouraging this enterprise. I also wish to thank the authors of these chapters for their seriousness of purpose and dedication to this work. Finally, I am grateful to Eliot Werner of Plenum Press for his aggressive, yet patient, and always witty supervision of the project.

MAUREEN T. HALLINAN

Contents

Chapter 3

Chapter 4

Chapter 5

Chapter 6

Chapter 7

Chapter 8

Chapter 9

CHAPTER 1

The Social Organization
of Schools

An Overview

MAUREEN T. HALLINAN

The aim of this book is to present, in a systematic manner, the most recent theoretical formulations on school organization and schooling processes. Much of the previous research in sociology of education has been empirical and atheorctical; few major theoretical analyses of educational issues can be found in the literature. The theoretical work that does exist is generally found in discrete papers and rarely brought together with other theoretical contributions on the same or related topics. Rarely does a group of sociologists identify an important topic in education and jointly attempt to conceptualize the issues related to that topic, each from his or her own perspective. A unique feature of this volume is that the primary goal of the authors of all the chapters was to conceptualize the schooling process and to present new theoretical models of how schools operate.

A second distinguishing characteristic of the volume is its focus on the social organization of the school and its effects on

Maureen T. Hallinan • Department of Sociology, University of Notre Dame, Notre Dame, IN 46556.

student outcomes. This is a fairly recent perspective on the study of schools. Major earlier research traditions include the production function studies (e.g., Coleman *et al.*, 1966) that examined the effects of educational resources and climate on academic achievement and educational attainment and the status attainment research (e.g., Sewell, Haller, and Portes, 1969; Sewell and Hauser, 1975) that investigated how ascribed and achieved characteristics of students and of their schools influence their educational aspirations and attainment and in turn their occupational status and income. Neither of these perspectives was concerned with school organization or the dynamics of how students learn in school. Reviews of these and other more psychological approaches to the study of schools are found in Barr and Dreeben (1983) and Hallinan (1985).

Concern with the social organization of schools is of fundamental concern and importance to sociologists of education. The purpose of schooling is to expose students to knowledge or information. That is, schools are established to present information to students and to facilitate their learning it. The study of the social organization of schools addresses a number of questions related to the process of transmitting knowledge to students. Among these questions are the following: what bodies of knowledge are presented to students in school; are students differentially exposed to information based on their ascribed or achieved characteristics; and in what context is knowledge presented?

Although at first glance these issues may seem to be instructional in nature, they are actually much broader than a narrow concern with curriculum content and methods of instruction. Investigations into the social organization of schools reveal that the way in which students are distributed across educational resources, including schools, tracks, grades, classrooms, and ability groups, and the context in which instruction takes place, are key determinants of what students learn in school.

The three main components of the social organization of the school are the curriculum, the assignment process, and the environment. By affecting the amount and kind of information to which a student is exposed, these three components represent important determinants of educational opportunity. The mechanisms that relate these factors to learning will now be discussed.

THE ORGANIZATION OF KNOWLEDGE: THE CURRICULUM

The curriculum is the body of knowledge or information that is presented to students in school. The content of the curriculum is usually determined outside of the classroom, by district or school-level authorities, often in collaboration with school boards or committees established for this purpose. Decisions regarding the content of the curriculum vary across school districts and even across schools within a district. An interesting consequence of this variation is that the knowledge to which a student is exposed in school is determined, in part at least, by what school the student attends.

Researchers have studied the curriculum from a number of different perspectives. A major interest has been how the curriculum is transmitted to students. This concern has stimulated numerous studies on the effectiveness of methods of instruction as well as some interest in instructional materials. Researchers also have examined and evaluated efforts at curriculum reform such as the move to diversify the curriculum, the "back to basics" movement, Head Start programs, Chapter I programs, and the like. Another focus of study has been what Jackson (1968) calls "the hidden curriculum," that is, the socialization of students to the kinds of behavior that school authorities define as appropriate for school. Others examine the curriculum from a broader perspective, namely, as a way of socializing students to the dominant values and norms of the society in which the school operates.

In contrast to these perspectives, the approach to the curriculum taken in this volume is to view it as part of the organization of the school. An elaboration of this perspective is found in Barr and Dreeben (1983) and is reflected in the chapter by these authors and by others in this volume. It will be outlined briefly here.

Decisions regarding the content of the curriculum for a particular school district or school are made in response to a number of factors, including tradition, community values, and the needs and preferences of the student population. Once the content of a curriculum has been established, school personnel decide how it will be organized for transmission to the students. The organization of the curriculum involves subdividing it into subject areas and courses. This is done in such a way as to correspond with the organizational differentiation of students for instruction. In secondary schools, the first level of curriculum differentiation usually is the selection of subject areas and courses for academic, vocational, and general tracks. Within this structure, the curriculum is further subdivided in those schools that have tracks or ability groups. Subject areas and courses are defined, for example, for advanced placement students and for those who need remedial work. At the middle and elementary levels, curriculum differentiation ordinarily occurs when students are assigned to ability groups for instruction. Consequently, students are exposed to different knowledge depending on the track or group to which they have been assigned for instruction.

Even when the same curriculum is established for different instructional groups, differences can occur across groups in the amount of knowledge the students receive. These differences result from variation in the level at which the material is presented, the rate of presentation, the types of materials used, the amount of instructional time provided, and the climate of instruction. There is considerable evidence, for example, that although elementary school teachers tend to distribute their time fairly evenly across ability groups, they provide instruction of lower quality and spend less time on instruction in low-ability groups than in middle or high groups (e.g., Good and Marshall, 1984; Eder, 1981). Moreover, teachers use a variety of textbooks and other educational materials which differ in level of interest, in relevance for the pupils, in clarity of exposition, and in level of difficulty. Materials that are too difficult or flawed from a pedagogical standpoint deter the transmission of the curriculum to students whereas effective materials facilitate learning.

Viewing the curriculum as an organizational feature of the school underscores the fact that the curriculum and its organization are the primary determinants of what information students receive in school. In the past, the curriculum was viewed as a static feature of a school. But an organizational perspective suggests that the transmission of the curriculum to the student body is a dynamic process which has a strong impact on what students learn in school. Decisions made by school personnel regarding instructional grouping, scheduling, selection of textbooks and materials, and assignment of teachers determine what part of the curriculum is transmitted to which students and with what effectiveness. Consequently, differences in curriculum organization result in a differentiation of the student body according to the amount or type of knowledge that different segments receive.

THE ORGANIZATION OF STUDENTS: THE ASSIGNMENT PROCESS

Intimately connected to the organization of the curriculum is the organization of students for instruction. The organizational differentiation of students in school structures educational opportunities for students (Sørensen, 1970). In the first place, organizational differentiation affects how and what part of the curriculum is channeled to students. Moreover, assignment to instructional groups determines the content, rate, and duration of instruction as well as the climate in which learning occurs. In the short run instructional grouping practices constrain students' opportunities to learn as they progress through their school careers, and in the long run they influence students' educational attainment.

The most obvious student characteristic considered by school authorities as they assign pupils to instructional groups is student aptitude or ability. Since many educators believe that instruction is most effective when the learners are homogeneous with respect to aptitude, grouping students by ability is a popular pedagogical practice. At the secondary level, ability grouping usually takes place across classes in the form of tracking. At the elementary level, it usually occurs within the classroom, with the class being subdivided by ability for instruction. The middle school often contains a combination of tracking and within-class ability grouping.

The basis for tracking or ability grouping is determined by the school principal and faculty; students are seldom given discretion in selecting a particular track. Pupils generally are assigned to tracks based on one or more of the following criteria: (1) standardized achievement test scores, (2) grades on class tests, (3) teacher and counselor recommendations, and (4) teacher evaluations of student maturity, seriousness of purpose, and behavior. In addition, there is a fairly widespread belief that, in some schools at least, assignment to tracks or ability groups is related to social class and ethnicity. This belief stems from the fact that a disproportionate number of low-income and minority students are found in the low tracks and ability groups in many schools in this country, whereas a greater proportion of higher-income and white students are assigned to the high tracks or ability groups.

The academic consequences of tracking and ability grouping appear to stem from differences in the quality and pace of instruction across different groups. Students in the upper tracks or ability groups are often taught by more experienced or popular teachers, cover more material and are exposed to a greater variety of interesting pedagogical practices. Students in the low tracks or ability groups often receive instruction that is repetitive, slow-paced, and unchallenging. These differences directly affect students' achievement, motivation, aspirations, and self-esteem.

Further consequences of tracking and ability grouping occur because the assignment process tends to be fairly stable. Once students are assigned to a particular track or ability group, they generally remain there for the duration of the school year or even, as is frequently the case, for their entire school career. This is partly for organizational ease, but, more importantly, it is a result of the content and pace of instruction to which students are exposed in different tracks or ability groups. Students in the lower tracks or ability groups are usually not encouraged or permitted to change groups because they are ill-prepared for courses requiring higher aptitude or a stronger background in the subject area. As a result, the options available to students in low-ability groups or tracks become more limited as they advance through school. Indeed, courses that are required for admission to institutions of higher education may simply be out of the range of possibility for these students because of the sequence of courses to which they were assigned earlier in their schooling.

Schools also attempt to accommodate students' interests and talents in the assignment process. One way they do this is by providing a variety of curricular areas and courses from which students may choose electives. Secondary schools offer diverse curricular and course opportunities, but more limited opportunities for choice are provided in the middle school and virtually no choice is available at the elementary level.

Factors that govern students' choice in selecting curriculum areas and courses in secondary schools are also part of the study of the social organization of schools. Among these factors are (1) background characteristics, (2) a student's prior history of curricular assignments and course selections, (3) teacher and counselor guidance, (4) parental advice, and (5) peer influences. Consequences of these self-selections are similar to those of tracking and ability grouping in that they can either create opportunities for a wide array of choices at a future point in a student's educational career or they can foreclose future opportunities by not providing students with the training needed for advanced courses or courses in different curricular areas. For example, the reluctance of female students to select advanced mathematics courses in middle and secondary school, likely due to peer pressure or the absence of role models, has serious implications for their future learning opportunities and careers in mathematics and science. Consequently, identifying the factors that lead to course selection is of critical importance in understanding the assignment process and intervening in the process when appropriate.

Given the serious consequences of tracking and curricular choices for students' cognitive and social development and for their future educational and career opportunities, systematic research is needed on the processes that govern the assignment of students to tracks and ability groups and influence student decisions regarding course selections. The theoretical models presented in this volume represent a major contribution to this end.

THE ORGANIZATION OF THE ENVIRONMENT: SCHOOL, COMMUNITY, AND SOCIETY

Although the organization of the curriculum and the organizational differentiation of students for instruction are major determinants of student learning, the impact of these factors is determined or modified, often in a dramatic way, by the context or environment in which learning takes place. There are three aspects of the school environment that affect the learning process: the school climate, the community or network of persons connected to the school, and the larger society in which the school is located. Each of these components of the school environment affects what students are taught in school and the relevance pupils attach to different aspects of the curriculum.

The society or culture in which a school is located defines the meaning of schooling and the importance of its outcomes. Some see the school as a response to the needs of society for technological growth and development. Others view the school as preparing students for society's competition for wealth, power, and prestige. In either case, schools are affected by the institutionalized set of rules that govern the educational system within a country. These rules provide the chartering privilege of the school and define requirements for graduation, diplomas, and degrees.

In Chapter 7 of this volume, Meyer argues that the institutionalized rules governing education affect the definition of the curriculum and the assignment of students to instructional groups in schools. An implication of this argument is that the basic conservatism evident in the curriculum of most schools, in this country and elsewhere, as well as in methods of organizing students for instruction, arises from the school's response to the institutionalized rules of education. This view portrays the social organization of the school as determined by the organization and value system of society and depicts the organization of the institution of education as the appropriate object of efforts toward educational reform.

The organization of the community in which a school is located also has a strong influence on the learning process. Some attention has been given to this influence on schooling in the past. For example, a body of research exists on parent–school relationships and the effects of parental involvement on a child's success in school. Research is also available that examines the effects of community involvement in school issues on the establishment of school policy. A number of studies examine school–community controversies, such as the busing issue, textbook controversies, and the establishment of educational programs such as special education, bilingual education, and athletic programs.

Another perspective on school–community relations is presented by network theorists. They have examined how characteristics of the network of school–community relations affect school practices and student outcomes. Coleman's analysis of the relationship between school and community in Chapter 8 of this volume falls within this perspective. He conceptualizes the school as an organization with an identifiable structure and with a network of ties to the community that it serves. Characteristics of the network such as its density and its intergenerational closure are seen as having important effects on student learning. These effects are transmitted by the position parents occupy in the network and by the links existing among parents and teachers.

An important defining feature of the climate of a school is the set of values, norms, and standards of behavior that teachers present to the students. This is referred to as moral education. Moral education may be included as a formal part of the curriculum, for example, in the social studies curriculum or as a unit on civic education, or, in religiously affiliated schools, in a religion syllabus. Even when moral education is not formally taught, however, it is still a dimension of schooling. Moral education, or the transmission of values and norms regarding behavior in and out of school, most frequently takes place through social interactions between teachers and students and among students themselves.

Since the assignment of students to instructional groupings determines the pool of adults and peers with whom a student interacts, this aspect of the organization of the school has a powerful impact on the type of moral education a student receives. The values teachers emphasize and communicate may vary across ability groups. For example, teachers may feel that for students in high-ability tracks or instructional groups progress in school work is more important than developing social skills. In contrast, they may assume that for students in low-ability tracks or groups discipline deserves more attention than learning. Peer pressure is likely to reinforce some of these attitudes. As a result, high-ability students may be taught a different set of values and norms than their lower-aptitude classmates.

In addition, the school provides the context in which students interact and the set of issues about which students must make moral judgments. These issues differ across schools. They may also differ by student cohort within a school. Variations in these issues result in different learning experiences for students. One consequence of these differences is the distinct student subcultures that emerge in different schools or within the same school.

Other characteristics of the school environment also affect the nature of moral education. The distribution of ascribed and achieved characteristics in a faculty, for example, is an important determinant of the school environment. A socially homogeneous faculty is more likely to adhere to and transmit to the students a uniform set of values and norms than a faculty that is more heterogeneous with respect to religious affiliation, social status, income, or educational attainment. The same is true of the social homogeneity of the student body. Nevertheless, even when a faculty or student body is fairly heterogeneous with respect to values and norms, the organizational differentiation of students within a school can produce a more homogeneous environment for subsets of students, resulting in the school's having a strong impact on the formation of their values and moral judgments.

In Chapter 9 of this volume, Bidwell conceptualizes the relationship between a school's context or environment, as determined by its social organization, and moral education. He argues that the organization of the curriculum and of the faculty and student body affects the transmission of values to students and the formation of their moral judgments. These, in turn, influence student commitments and social behavior. The school, then, is viewed as the context in which moral education takes place, with variations across schools occurring because of differences in organizational features of schools.

In general, conceptualizing learning as a process conditioned by the social organization of the school sheds considerable light on what and how students learn in school. The theoretical formulations presented in this volume describe the mechanisms linking school organization to learning. This perspective allows us to move beyond earlier naive notions about what makes a school effective. School resources or composition are not the primary determinants of school effects, nor is student learning determined only by social origins and student background characteristics. Rather, the study of the social organization of schools indicates that schools are effective in promoting student learning to the extent that they make appropriate decisions governing the school curriculum, the organizational differentiation of students for instruction, and the nature of the school environment.

REFERENCES

Barr, Rebecca and Robert Dreeben. 1983. *How Schools Work*. Chicago: University of Chicago Press.

Coleman, James S., E. Q. Campbell, C. J. Hobson, J. McPartland, A. M. Mood, F. Weinfield and R. L. York. 1966. *Equality of Educational Opportunity*. Washington, D.C.: U.S. Government Printing Office.

Eder, Donna. 1981. "Ability grouping as a self-fulfilling prophecy: a microanalysis of teacher–student interaction." *Sociology of Education* 54:151–161.

Good, Thomas L. and Susan Marshall. 1984. "Do students learn more in heterogeneous or homogeneous groups?" Chapter 2 (pp. 15–38) in Penelope L. Peterson, Louise Cherry Wilkinson and Maureen T. Hallinan (eds.), *The Social Context of Instruction*. Orlando, Florida: Academic Press.

Hallinan, Maureen T. 1985. "Sociology of education: the state of the art." Chapter 1 (pp. 33–51) in Jeanne H. Ballantine (ed.), *Schools and Society*. Palo Alto, California: Mayfield.

Jackson, Philip W. 1968. *Life in the Classroom*. New York: Holt, Rinehart and Winston.

Sewell, William H., Archibald O. Haller, and Alejandro Portes. 1969. "The educational and early occupational attainment process." *American Sociological Review* 34:82–91.

Sewell, William H. and Robert M. Hauser. 1975. *Education, Occupation and Earnings; Achievement in the Early Career*. New York: Academic Press.

Sørensen, Aage B. 1970. "Organizational differentiation of students and educational opportunity." *Sociology of Education* 43:355–376.

CHAPTER 2

An Organizational Analysis of Curriculum and Instruction

ROBERT DREEBEN and REBECCA BARR

The purpose of this chapter is to treat the curriculum as part of school system organization and to establish its link to the technology of instruction. It will not deal with individual achievement or with the connection between schools and society but rather will address the question of how the curriculum can be seen as an organizational force, hitherto neglected, that drives the school's technology—classroom instruction.

Our understanding of the schools and their effects since the 1960s has been strongly influenced by a public policy agenda that has placed great stress on educational resources and on social psychological considerations of status that bear on the equality of educational outcomes. These outcomes, moreover,

Robert Dreeben • Department of Education, University of Chicago, Chicago, IL 60637.   **Rebecca Barr** • National College of Education, Evanston, IL 60201. The work reported here is based on a Project on Classroom Organization, Instruction, and Learning generously supported by the Spencer Foundation, and that support is gratefully acknowledged.

have been construed in a rather disembodied way—as achievement measured by achievement tests with little attention devoted
to the substance of what is learned. None of these considerations draws much attention to the schools' conventional task
of transmitting through instruction the knowledge contained
in the curriculum.

Schools exist to transmit knowledge to individuals. The
consequences of doing so shape the larger society. A political
understanding of this contention has stimulated the examination of how the history, civics, and social studies curricula, as
well as the experience of schooling generally, contribute to the
transmission of national tradition, to civic consciousness, to
political participation and a sense of civic responsibility, and to
support for the form of government (Easton and Dennis, 1969;
Janowitz, 1983; Jennings and Niemi, 1974; Merriam, 1931).

Interest in the curricular impact of schooling, however, is
not limited to the political realm. It extends to questions of
social cleavage and the continuance of economic inequality in
society through the reproduction of culture and relations of
class dominance (Apple, 1979, 1982; Carnoy and Levin, 1985;
Young, 1971). It is curious that recent sociological interest in
the curriculum has been largely preempted by Marxian
approaches, although not completely monopolized by them
(Alexander and Cook, 1982; Meyer, 1977). Curricular questions
are by no means limited to the problem of social reproduction.

While treatment of the curriculum has been mostly macrosociological, the last two decades have seen the publication of
cross-national studies by the IEA measuring knowledge in different subject areas at the individual level (Comber and Keeves,
1973; Husen, 1967; Torney, Oppenheim, and Farnen, 1975).
The argument of these largely psychological studies is essentially the reverse of the social and political ones noted above.
They examine the effects of national characteristics, including
those of school systems, on subject matter learning.

What is common to both agendas is that the nature and
contribution of the schools themselves are largely omitted. In
the first case, the aggregated impact of individuals' knowledge,

beliefs, actions, and attitudes is presumably what shapes the larger society. Only the reproductionist view that school organization reflects the social relations of production has so far provided a link, however unpersuasive, between the individual and the larger society. In the second case, the links between society, the schools, and individuals are rarely described. Teacher assessments of student opportunities to learn subjects and global indices of school properties are left to carry the explanatory burden.

The starting point of this paper is our earlier work (Barr and Dreeben, 1983) showing coverage of curricular material to be a component of elementary school reading instruction. We viewed coverage as a phenomenon tied to reading groups. This was because in the course of reading instruction all students in the same reading group, despite individual differences, covered the same amount of material. Although students in each group learned different amounts and differed from each other in aptitude and in other respects, the instruction they received was not geared to these variations. Teachers taught the groups they created and taught individuals as a by-product of that.

Treating coverage as a form of mediation between grouping and individual learning emphasizes the social psychological meaning of that concept. It is the mechanism by which a property of school social organization—instructional groups—is transformed into individual experience. By virtue of their membership, all students in the group undergo uniform treatment: read the same material at the same time with the same teacher before the same audience. What happens to that common experience when it enters each student's mind differs among members of the same group. That is why learning differs among group members even after the effects of common treatment on that learning have been taken into account.

Although that work also identified the determinants (the mean aptitude of groups, the difficulty of learning materials, and the availability of time) as well as the effects of group coverage, it conceptualized coverage primarily as the *use* of educational resources—learning material and time—for their impact on individual learning. What coverage represents at the higher levels of school district organization was not pursued systematically except to note that materials usually enter the school system through the central administrative office and occasionally at the school and class levels.

This chapter explores the concept of coverage in order to understand the place of the curriculum in the social organization of school systems. Coverage has two components. The first pertains to *what* is covered (that is, content); the second pertains to *how much* is covered. In the pages to follow we view the curriculum as an element of the social organization of school systems and also argue that it represents a driving force in their operation.

THE CURRICULUM AS AN ORGANIZATIONAL PROPERTY

What is the curriculum and what are its parts? The most direct answer is that it represents bodies of knowledge and skills deemed worth imparting. That explicit meaning can be tied to documentary evidence available in any school district. Other meanings, however, cannot be tied down so directly. Some knowledge and skills, for example, are learned without being taught. They are products of schools' being organized in particular ways and of their providing certain experiences that may not have been designed to have an explicit educative impact. These less direct effects of schooling can be called curricular— some years ago they were called the hidden curriculum—but they do not pertain except indirectly to school programs built around subject matter. Schools also try to create an ambiance or atmosphere, internal outcomes that cannot properly be called knowledge. Even though these more evanescent outcomes are not explicitly formulated in a course of study or conveyed directly through instruction, they have a curricular component because they are believed to affect student knowledge, conduct, and adherence to social norms. This chapter, however, will restrict itself to the formal curriculum embodied in tangible curricular materials used for instruction.

Curriculum content, from time to time and place to place, is a perennial topic of intellectual, philosophical, and political controversy. Although curricular controversy is never resolved in any final sense, school systems in the near term must either establish programs of study in the central administration or else devolve them to schools or to teachers. Whatever the locus of binding curricular decisions, they must be made; otherwise the schools have no knowledge to impart.

Centralized curricular decisions are common and usually entail the acquisition of textbooks and other materials deemed appropriate to each subject and grade. Although textbook content—even in school districts that rely heavily on them—does not exhaust the question of what is deemed worth knowing, it usually preempts a large portion of it. Whatever else is taken to be worth knowing enters the curriculum through supplementation to provide for the needs of special subpopulations of students and to permit the expression of personal teaching styles and agendas.

Although the books selected embody curricular priorities, what stands behind the selection is a claim that the priorities are justifiable, at least over the short term (such as the customary five-year period separating successive textbook reviews). The curriculum, along with other elements of the school system's agenda, such as the calendar and the schedule, must be found acceptable to the community of taxpayers and parents and to the system's administrative and instructional employees.

Although crises of legitimacy are more the exception than the rule, the fact that public controversies do arise, for example, over the suitability of Darwinian theory, *Man: A Course of Study*, *Huckleberry Finn*, sex education, and school prayer indicates that commitments to teach certain kinds of knowledge, even if sanctioned on intellectual and pedagogical grounds, cannot be taken for granted among those who support the school system.

Similarly, the community of professional educators, especially teachers, must also find the curriculum acceptable according to intellectual criteria and pedagogical standards of good practice. The crises of confidence over the new math and the *Chicago Mastery Learning Reading* materials, for example, indicate that teachers entrusted with imparting the curriculum must find it both within their power to teach and consistent with their good judgment about what is worth teaching. Otherwise, inappropriate materials or teachers' half-hearted engagement will undermine instruction.

In the literature on educational effects, little or no attention has been devoted to what directs school systems' internal activities and sustains them on a continuing basis. What, in other words, makes a school system go, what is the driving force? In the private industrial and commercial sectors of the economy, motivations to make a profit or increase market share are large parts of the picture, though by themselves insufficient explanations. Commitments to particular goods or services of given quality must also be present. Not-for-profit enterprises, like school systems, must rely heavily on commitments. The curriculum, we believe, is the focus of such commitments, and it is one that contributes to explaining how and why schools operate on a continuing basis.

We will argue that when school systems adopt curricular programs they not only claim their appropriateness but also commit themselves to transmitting the content to students, that is, to having students "cover" the material in order to learn it. In concrete terms, this means engaging students with the content that books and other materials contain. In order for this to happen, teachers must organize much, and sometimes all, of their instruction around the content presented in the adopted textbooks and design their instruction so that some amount of that material becomes the academic agenda for a school year.

The curriculum as an organizational phenomenon represents an agenda of work. And although it exerts an obligatory force on teachers, partly because representatives of the teaching force often contribute to district-wide decisions about book adoptions, its influence is also subject to contingencies. For example, if a single text is adopted for eighth-grade math, its content, in whole or in part, will be the heart of the curriculum for the year. The teacher's job is to get through it. Getting through it, however, might not be possible for a variety of reasons: not enough time has been allocated in the schedule, some portion or all of the class might not be prepared to deal with the difficulty of the problems, or the teacher might use time poorly. Similarly, getting through the material might be possible, but for a variety of reasons it does not happen (Barr, 1985b). In schools and classrooms, the curriculum as an organizational resource becomes entangled with prevailing constraints in the school system: student abilities, time, teacher abilities and preferences, and the like.

We have argued so far that schooling is driven by commitments established by the board of education, which certifies to the community that the curriculum is appropriate, that it conforms to professional pedagogical standards, and that its content is intellectually defensible. The curriculum now rests in the hands of those who implement it—administrators and teachers. It is entirely possible that a dispassionate observer might find these certifications unwarranted, but that is not the point. What matters is that the school system operates according to such commitments.

Our empirical analysis attempts to explain how general curricular commitments become transformed into resource allocations and patterns of resource use that in turn shape group instruction: the amount of curricular material covered by teachers in their instruction of reading groups. We know from our current work in first grade that covering material in groups is strongly related to both word learning ($r = 0.94$) and general first-grade reading achievement ($r = .76$; Dreeben and Gamoran, 1985). And although instruction itself is the dependent variable in this analysis, its salient characteristic is its strong influence on learning.

DESCRIPTION OF THE STUDY

The evidence we present was collected as part of a larger project on the social organization of schools. Data were gathered (1981–82 and 1982–83 school years) through testing and classroom observation of the resources available in schools (time, curricular materials, teacher activities, student characteristics, and the social and ability composition of classes and instructional groups), and on their use in instruction. In three Chicago metropolitan area districts we studied seven schools and within them 13 classes, 50 instructional groups, and over 300 first-graders.

We observed each class 12 times over the school year (at roughly three-week intervals) for a full day and paid special attention to the nature and duration of activities that comprised reading instruction. We documented the amount of curricular material presented, the composition of reading groups, and the difficulty of the reading curriculum. This paper draws upon the characteristics of the 50 reading groups as composed at the time of the tenth classroom observation in mid-April.[1]

We begin with an attempt to identify what a general commitment to the curriculum means and then turn to the question of how it is embodied in the use of time in reading activities and how it is influenced by contingencies related to the properties of reading groups.

We found two main indications of curricular commitment. The first pertains to the acquisition of curricular materials by the district or to the district's approval (through an approved

[1]The choice of the tenth observation was made for technical reasons. In general, the groups are fairly stable over time, even though there is a certain amount of individual mobility up and down and changes in group arrangements in the classes. The tenth observation provides a representative picture of group organization. It comes late enough in the year to be past the more fluid period of group formation in the fall; and with the exception of one class that reorganized itself for the eleventh and twelfth observations, the tenth observation provides a good picture of things prevailing at the twelfth (and last) observation.

list) of materials acquired by schools or teachers. The second pertains to establishing time guidelines and then time allocations for covering content.

Curricular Materials

The reading curriculum is designed to support reading development from readiness in the kindergarten to fairly well developed reading proficiency in the upper intermediate grades. The curricular package consists of a set of related materials, some to be read by students and some by teachers. Student materials include the basal readers composed of stories, poems, and articles; workbook exercises, frequently coordinated with the basal selections and usually completed independently as seatwork; and supplementary worksheets and story books to be assigned at the teacher's discretion. The teacher's manual includes a discussion of the philosophy of the program and its organization and specific suggestions for the goals and activities of lessons.

The materials are designed to increase in difficulty from level to level in the program. Word identification and comprehension skills, sight vocabulary, and reading strategies developed at one level prepare children for the stories and workbook exercises at the next. The sequential levels of material are somewhat arbitrarily defined, but almost all programs discuss which levels are appropriate for specific grades. This grading sets expectations for what constitutes grade-appropriate work and also establishes a division of labor among teachers. That is, teachers assume responsibility for introducing grade-level materials but often hesitate to have children work on materials designated as above grade unless such acceleration is approved by other teachers and the school administration.

Curricular materials may be selected by district-level committees or alternatively by schools or individual teachers. In the three districts we studied, decisions about reading programs were made at the district level. In Districts II and III, committees of teachers and administrators were appointed every five years to study alternatives and to recommend a program for adoption. District II selected the *HBJ Bookmark Reading Program* (1979). As shown in Table 1, the first-grade portion of that program included basal readers with 96 story lessons that introduced 444 different words.

District III selected the *Houghton Mifflin Reading Series* (1976). Table 1 shows this program to be more demanding, not only because it includes more stories (105) and more words (716) but also because the ratio of new words to stories read is greater than that in the District II program. This means that the program provides less practice per word. In the selection of a basal

Table 1
Characteristics of Curricular Materials

District, school, and class	Class mean aptitude	Reading materials		Content coverage in words[a]
		Stories	Words	
I/A/1[c]	26.6	70	490	391–429[b]
I/A/2	29.6	70	490	190–657
I/B/3	12.2	90	544	86–381[b]
I/B/4	22.7	93	593	93–441[b]
I/G/13	19.0	60	388	46–344
II/C/5	12.0	96	444	162–381
II/C/6	16.2	96	444	140–342
II/D/7	18.8	96	444	186–444
II/D/8	17.7	96	444	186–444
III/E/9	32.1	105	716	513–614
III/E/10	33.4	105	716	394–614[b]
III/F/11	29.6	105	716	623–806
III/F/12	28.5	105	716	623–806

[a]Refers to the range in the number of words covered between the low and high groups in the class.

[b]In some classes there were groups with special circumstances that account for uncharacteristic rates of coverage. In Schools A and B, either group members were bilingual or the groups were formed late in the year. Class 1 contained a group with coverage of 331; Class 3 contained a group with coverage of 31; Class 4 contained a group with coverage of 16; Class 10 contained a group of repeaters from the previous year with coverage of 950.

[c]Number of words contained in the District I materials consists of the sum of those in basal readers and in the CMLR materials less the overlapping words.

series, in other words, the district defines what the content of the reading curriculum will be, sets expectations for what should be covered, and creates contingencies for classroom teachers that can affect the design of instruction and learning.

District I, rather than selecting a single basal program, established a list of approved programs from which schools, or even teachers, could select. Each school in District I adopted a different series: School A used the *The Bank Street Reading Series* (1966); School B, a portion of an earlier program developed by Houghton Mifflin (1971); and School G, the Ginn reading program, *Reading 720* (1979).

In addition, District I also mandated a reading skills program, *Chicago Mastery Learning Reading* (1981), and required teachers to spend an hour a day teaching the concepts it contained. Unfortunately, these materials are designed with little contextual reading. Since teachers in the sample were aware that story reading is necessary to insure the incorporation of reading skills, particularly at the first-grade level, all taught reading with the basal programs as well as with CMLR.

The information in Table 1 about the characteristics of first-grade reading materials combines the number of different words from the two sets of materials. It shows that the number of words introduced in Schools A and B is greater than in District II, but fewer stories are available to consolidate the learning of words. Teacher 13 in School G used materials that introduced few words and relatively little story reading.

Table 1 also includes the mean reading aptitude of each class. Although it is true that District III with the most able classes used the most difficult reading program, the relation between the difficulty of materials and class ability is not so clear in Districts I and II. For example, School A with the most able classes used slightly more demanding materials than those used in District II but not than those in School B. Generally, however, the correlation between class mean aptitude and the number of words introduced in first-grade materials is high ($r = .73$).

With this description of the reading curricula in mind, we

proceed to how the curriculum influences classroom instruction. Although district and/or school decisions about the curriculum might directly determine the content of instruction, it is important to recall the distinction between what is introduced and how much is covered. There is little question that the curriculum exerts a decisive influence on what is taught. Close adherence to the reading curriculum is not so surprising in the case of District I, where teachers used the CMLR materials to enable their students to pass the criterion-referenced tests monitored closely by district administrators. But in all districts teachers introduced the basal reading selections lesson by lesson with no omissions even in the absence of close administrative monitoring.

Although it can be shown that the content of the reading curriculum generally determines what is taught, not all groups covered all the materials identified as first-grade work. Table 1 indicates how much of the materials was actually read by the lowest and highest ability groups in the 13 classes by mid-May of first grade. The highest group in Class 1, for example, completed a 429-word portion of the total curriculum; the lowest group was not far behind, having read stories composed of 391 different words.

The table indicates that commitment to the curriculum does not determine precisely how much of the curriculum is taught. Coverage varies among groups in each class because teachers adjust their assignments to the aptitude levels of their reading groups. Further, differences exist between teachers within schools. With the exception of School B, classes in schools tend to be similar in aptitude and use the same curricular programs. Thus, variations between teachers in other schools arise mainly from differences in teacher preferences and style.

More interesting than the differences within classes that clearly reflect grouping, and between teachers within schools that reflect teacher style, are those between districts and schools. Table 1 shows that all groups, even the lowest, in District III complete more reading lessons than most groups in the other districts. These findings suggest that more demanding reading programs, selected with the participation of teachers at the district level (or directly selected by teachers), promote greater coverage among low-aptitude as well as high-aptitude groups. That is, a difficult program establishes not only high expectations for able students but extremely high expectations for less able ones as well. The relation, however, may not be simple: districts with more "ready" students tend to select more difficult programs (see Table 1); further, it may be that districts selecting more difficult materials spend more time in covering them.

The general pattern does not hold for all cases. School B, for example, employs very demanding basal materials but does not realize high coverage. This exceptional case exposes an assumption that underlies our view that curricular commitments drive the instructional apparatus of school systems. We believe that the view holds when there are orderly connections among the components of school organization: materials generally appropriate to the ability levels of students, time provided to accord with the demands of the curriculum, curricular materials that are mutually consistent (unlike the combination of CMLR and basal materials), and administrative oversight of the connection between curriculum and instruction. In School B, none of these conditions obtained. In general, there is no *automatic* process by which curricular commitments set the rest of the organization in motion and that integrates its elements. As with any technological process of production, basic commitments will drive the system when thought and action are devoted to the connections among its parts.

We can conclude from this discussion that there is a substantial relation between the selection of a curricular program and how much is covered during reading instruction. The relation, however, holds on the average. The contents of the reading program appear to set expectations for what is to be covered particularly by the high-ability groups across classes in a district. These expectations appear to extend to low-ability groups as well, though not as rigorously; for although students in low groups in a district with a demanding curriculum do not cover as much as their high group counterparts, they still cover more

than high groups in other districts with less demanding programs. Even so, the program does not establish rigid upper
limits; three teachers in our sample exceeded the contents of
the materials designated for the first grade by proceeding to
the second-grade basal readers.

The Commitment of Time

The acquisition of materials by a school district represents
one manifestation of curricular commitment. This is especially
true for early elementary school reading which relies so heavily
on a text. The availability of materials, however, cannot by itself
constitute a commitment; time must be set aside for their use,
and they must actually be used.

As part of their obligations to the state as agencies of public
instruction, school boards determine the length of the school
day. That length of time, spread over a school year, sets the
upper limit on what is available for all subjects. Whereas the
state regulates in a general way, school districts do so precisely.
As Table 2 indicates, Districts I, II, and III set their school bells
at 297, 305, and 335 minutes, respectively, times that represent
the length of the school day (excluding lunch). District policies
account for school day differences of nearly 40 minutes. It
remains to be seen how such general time allocations become
specified into curricular priorities for reading and into instructional time actually spent.

In addition to defining the length of the school day, districts also provide written guidelines for the amount of time to
be spent on reading and language arts, the most general des-
ignation for the curricular area that includes reading at the
elementary level. Districts I and III publish their guidelines: 820
and 700 (in a range of 600 to 800) minutes per week, respectively. District II does not publish a guideline but instead uses
a discontinued state guideline of 700 minutes per week within
a 650 to 750 minute range. The state no longer provides any
time guidelines for elementary-level curricular areas; it leaves
such matters up to the local districts.

Table 2
Time Guidelines and Allocations

	Daily time	Reading and language arts time	Whole-class reading time	Small group basal time	
				Low	High
District I					
Guideline	297	164			
School A					
Class 1	300.8	100.4	7.6	11.6	15.3
Class 2	299.1	147.7	11.0	10.6	15.6
School B					
Class 3	312.9	136.0	27.2	4.1	13.8
Class 4	303.7	148.3	24.8	5.3	7.7
School G					
Class 13	299.8	107.7	49.8	5.9	8.3
District II					
Guideline	305	140			
School C					
Class 5	304.3	135.1	6.2	22.3	28.2
Class 6	303.8	124.3	5.8	14.0	17.0
School D					
Class 7	296.3	150.5	21.3	22.4	23.6
Class 8	294.1	151.3	20.2	13.3	17.8
District III					
Guideline	335	140			
School E					
Class 9	328.3	176.0	9.1	17.0	23.1
Class 10	325.6	155.4	1.4	18.0	19.6
School F					
Class 11	336.6	175.3	4.6	28.3	33.6
Class 12	336.9	193.3	3.7	27.8	38.1

We cannot generalize about the inverse relation between length of school day and time assigned to reading and language arts. What is impressive is how widely districts differ in their time priorities, and the fact that a commitment to "more education," which is perhaps what the longer school day indicates, does not proportionally mandate time to be spent on reading and language arts.

A district's guidelines for time to be spent on this part of the curriculum apply to all its schools. As to the length of the school day, district standards bind the schools. However, it is one thing to set the school bells and another to get students into and out of class; one thing to have a curricular guideline for a district and another to allocate time in classes.

Although school bells indicate when all students are supposed to be in and out of class, administrators and teachers are more or less assiduous in getting students into class and keeping them there until the time is up. Table 2 indicates very small classroom (i.e., teacher) differences within schools (School B is the only exception) but some substantial school differences within districts: School C makes about 8 more minutes per day available than School D, and School F makes about 10 more minutes available than School E. Overall, district guidelines closely approximate how much daily time is actually available. School differences and teacher similarities within schools suggest the vigilance of principals in having classes start promptly and run to the end. Note that the contribution of the principal is important because 5 to 10 minutes per day adds to almost one period per week—to be multiplied by the number of weeks in the school year.

Although district guidelines for time to be spent in reading and language arts activities represent a signal to schools and teachers, only in the classroom does a standard take concrete form as a time allocation. Time for reading and language arts represents a composite time allotment to activities that include basal and phonics instruction, writing, and spelling in all settings—small group, whole class, and individual—as well as time allocated for instruction but not actually used for it (e.g., time spent in transitions between activities, time spent in giving directions, and time wasted). It is a classroom measure distinct from the district guideline for reading and language arts.

Table 2 shows that in District I the time teachers allocate to reading and language arts falls substantially (at best 15 minutes) below the district guideline. In District II, both classes in School D come in at the top of the recommended range, whereas in School C the classes come in close to the bottom and below. In District III, three classes exceed the maximum of the recommended range while one comes in several minutes below the maximum but well above the guideline. If we average the class variations within schools, there are marked school differences in each district. These differences, however, do not reflect school policy or the principal's attempt to achieve uniformity, since teacher differences within schools tend to be very large.

Teachers carry substantial responsibility in establishing curricular priorities. In School A, for example, the two teachers differ by almost 50 minutes per day—an extraordinary amount of time in general but also in light of their location in the same school, subject to the same district guidelines and with virtually the same amount of total daily time at their disposal. In School E, the teachers differ by slightly over 20 minutes per day and in School F by slightly under 20—again, very large differences. Teacher differences are minimal, by contrast, in School D.

Even though teachers vary greatly in their commitment, the overall pattern for reading and language arts tends to be consistent with district variations in the length of the school day. This is a matter that apparently engages the attention of principals given the similarity of teachers in the same school. Their commitments, however, are not consistent with each district's guidelines for reading and language arts. District I with the highest guideline had the smallest classroom time allocations; the opposite held in District III. To believe that reading is important does not require consulting some set of written guidelines; the sense of curricular priority in reading has been expressed in public pronouncements, in current debates, and in research priorities—it is in the air. What appears to make a difference, then, is that the school schedule makes time available to teachers.

Other areas of the curriculum must also be fit into the school day. Time allocations for math, science, social studies, and health, however, increase only slightly with longer school days. In short, the commitment of teachers to the reading and language arts component of the curriculum appears to be tied both to a sense of its great importance and to the feasibility of doing justice to the area. The long school day provides that feasibility.

Districts I and III represent interesting contrasts, their school days differing by more than half an hour. Although teachers in both districts allocate about the same amount of time each morning to reading and language arts (between 164 and 179 minutes in District I, between 160 and 165 minutes in District III), afternoon time allocations differ markedly (121 to 146 minutes in District I, 165 to 171 minutes in District III). Time devoted to math in both districts is similar (a class range of between 30 and 40 minutes a day in each); District III classes devoted from 5 to 15 more minutes to science, social studies, and health than District I and thereby used up some of the additional time provided by the longer day. Most of the additional time, then, goes to reading and language arts. Real-time allocations, as distinct from guidelines, give a curricular preference substance.

We emphasize in a different way the importance of teachers in establishing curricular commitments. Given district constraints governing the length of the school day, and whatever additional pressure is brought to bear by the school principal in stressing its full utilization, teachers still exert considerable control over the proportion of the day they devote to reading and language arts. District I teachers range from 33.4 to 49.4 percent in the proportion of the school day devoted to reading and language arts, and District II from 50.8 to 51.4 percent. Despite differences among its teachers, District III, with the longest school day, also spends the highest proportion of daily time on classroom reading and language arts (ranging from 47.7 to 57.4 percent). Thus, daily time alone does not explain the commitment to reading and language arts shown by District III teachers.

Time commitments are important primarily as expressions of curricular intent. Instruction, by contrast, represents the actual use of time to present materials, to put the curriculum into effect.

Reading instruction contains many components: discussing stories in a small group, doing phonics exercises independently as seatwork, reading silently, listening to stories being read to the whole class, and so forth. In this analysis we have taken one facet of reading instruction that we consider to be the core activity of the whole enterprise: reading the basal series in a small group under close teacher supervision. Of the total amount of time each teacher allocates to reading and language arts, how much is spent in supervised, small-group basal reading?

We report supervised basal time both for the group receiving the least time and that receiving the most time (this distinction does not correspond to high- and low-ability groups; sometimes the low, sometimes a middle, and sometimes the high gets the most or the least time.) In addition, we report the time each class spends daily in reading instruction in a whole-class format.

Table 2 shows substantial differences. First, district differences, Districts II and III versus District I, are large. This difference, however, must not be understood simply as the translation of a curricular priority into a real-time expenditure. Rather, it reflects District I's deep commitment to CMLR materials designed to be used with a whole-class instructional format. Grouped basal instruction was secondary, and for that reason the time spent in small-group instruction was small. It must be noted, however, that whole-class reading time was also limited in School A. This was because most students had already mastered the concepts contained in CMLR materials.

Second, one school is highly mobilized for reading instruction (School F). District III provides a long school day; but although the teachers differ by 18 minutes in the time they set aside for reading and language arts, both devote almost equally substantial amounts of time for supervised, small-group basal instruction and considerably more than the teachers in School E of the same district. (The contrast between Teachers 9 and 11 is also instructive: similar reading and language-arts time commitments, very different time expenditures.) We cannot, of course, determine convincingly whether we are dealing just with teacher commitments and/or with the involvement of the school principal. Our evidence, however, points to the importance of the principal's contribution.

With our small numbers, we cannot claim to have provided a rigorous quantitative test of how general curricular commitments are transmitted through school-system organization and become realized in the use of instructional time. We have, however, provided evidence about how such a process works and where the sources of variation lie. Despite the small sample, large differences in commitment and time use have been found. Whether or not a larger and more rigorous analysis would demonstrate the dependence of teachers' curricular commitments on the amount of daily time the district makes available, the significance of teachers' time commitment and use in both constraining and opening up instructional opportunities, even within the same school, is undeniable.

CURRICULUM, TIME, AND GROUP CHARACTERISTICS

Time used for supervised basal reading in small groups, although an important element in the organization of instruction, does not by itself constitute curricular exposure. Two or more teachers, for example, can use the same amount of time to cover different amounts of material. Coverage itself represents real exposure within the constraints and opportunities established by time. In first-grade reading, the actual coverage of words and stories represents concretely the result of successive specifications of curricular commitments manifest both in materials and in time (the school year, in our study). How much variation in material covered in the 50 instructional groups can be accounted for as a consequence of curricular commitments and of their embodiment in time allocations? We address this question with a regression analysis.

As already discussed, commitments are expressed in the selection of materials and are represented by the number of words and stories contained in them (see Table 1). The length of the school day cannot appropriately be entered into a regression equation along with the number of new words introduced by the text because they are correlated at .90. Number of words is also correlated at .78 with reading and language arts time. In order to consider both time and materials as potential influences on coverage, basal supervised time, measured at the group level, must represent time commitment. Table 3 shows both measures of commitment to be significantly related to coverage: for number of words in the materials, beta = .34; for basal supervised time, beta = .55.

Independently of the time available for supervised basal instruction, the difficulty of materials is related to coverage. That is, the more words and stories there are to be covered, the more are indeed covered. Districts (and teachers with district approval) appear, in other words, to frame the curricular agenda—the amount of material they expect a substantial proportion of students to cover—over the whole year. At the same time, given the difficulty of the materials, the more time teachers provide for basal instruction out of their daily time allotment,

Table 3
Determinants of Content Coverage

	Coverage			
	B	b	se	p
Material difficulty	.34	.63	.20	.002
Basal supervised time	.55	14.26	2.74	.0001
R^2		.58		
R^2 adjusted		.57		
Material difficulty	.12	.23	.15	.13
Basal supervised time	.53	13.78	1.95	.0001
Group mean aptitude	.55	11.38	1.67	.0001
Group SD aptitude	.02	1.19	5.01	.81
Group size	.00	.11	5.91	.98
R^2		.85		
R^2 adjusted		.83		

the more words (and stories) are covered. That is, the more time they set aside for small-group basal instruction, the more of the curriculum they cover in that time.

Number of words in the material and basal supervised time together account for 58 percent of the variation in coverage. Just these two measures of curricular commitment in combination represent considerable influence on reading instruction. By themselves, however, they do not take into account the characteristics of the instructional groups that are created to regulate instruction according to differences in student ability. Accordingly, the higher the aptitude level of groups within classes, the more material is likely to be covered.

At the same time, because classes contain a diversity of student abilities, groups themselves vary in diversity. On the average, one would expect more diverse groups to be more difficult to instruct—and hence to cover less—than less diverse ones (though that is more likely to be true at the low end of the class distribution than at the high end). For a different reason, larger groups might cover less because more turns must be taken in a given amount of group time, and that time tends to be rather equally assigned to groups irrespective of their aptitude level.[2]

The evidence in Table 3 indicates that group mean aptitude is the largest determinant of coverage followed closely by basal supervised time. The two conditions we initially believed might inhibit coverage, group size and the group standard deviation of aptitude, were unrelated to it. Teachers, in short, create these groups and instruct them as created with group mean aptitude the guiding consideration that influences coverage, overriding the potential obstacles of size and diversity.

Number of words in the materials declines in importance

---

[2]We had anticipated that the more low-aptitude students there were in a group, the less the group would cover. Number of low aptitude students per group, however, was so highly related to mean aptitude that the two variables could not be treated in the same equation, and mean aptitude was conceptually the more important of the two.

after group mean aptitude is taken into account. That does not mean, however, that the content of the curriculum is unimportant as a determinant of coverage. The reason the coefficient for number of words declines when group mean aptitude is introduced is that the higher-aptitude groups in the whole sample of groups tend to be more highly concentrated in the same district (III) that uses the more demanding materials. The fact remains, however, that because a basal series is taken as a curricular agenda for the whole year, it is covered not only because it represents a commitment but because enough time is provided each day and cumulatively over the year to accommodate the burden of words and stories. In other words, both commitments and technological contingencies are involved.

SUMMARY

We conclude that the content of the reading curriculum establishes what is taught. What makes this statement more than a tautology is that the content contained in texts is taken by administrators and teachers as a curricular agenda. Whether the agenda is long or short, its content is spread over the year. In this manner, an expectation, or commitment, is created about the extent of the year's work. The difficulty of the curricular program, a matter settled at the district level, also influences, on the average, how much of the program is covered. Able as well as less able groups in the district using the most demanding materials covered more stories and words than those in other districts. Further, this influence occurred over and above that attributable to basal time allocations.

The influence of commitments may not be realized if the curriculum is inadequate or inappropriate to other class conditions such as the aptitude of students and time available for instruction. As we have shown, District I believed in good faith that the reading curriculum could best be implemented by using materials that turned out to have had palpable shortcomings. The directive to use these materials and the need to combine them with a basal program created difficulties for teachers in the management of instructional time. Just because there is a commitment does not mean it can or will be effectively implemented.

Districts also influence content coverage through their policies concerning time. Despite local variations in content and in centralized control, we found a cluster of time considerations that represent the means by which general curricular commitments are translated into specific instructional practices. The length of the school day sets an outside limit on the time available to each class for productive purposes. By contrast, general district commitments to time for language arts appear to have little bearing on what time actually is spent on language-arts activities.

The evidence shows, moreover, that teachers with both the longest school day and the most demanding materials allocate proportionately more of it to reading and language arts than did other teachers. If the demanding district-wide curricular commitment was to be met, time had to be provided in the class schedule. When difficult basal materials are employed, as in School B, where time is both short and preempted by a higher-priority nonbasal curriculum, very little basal material is covered.

One condition, shown to have a marked influence on basal coverage, is group mean aptitude. This influence reflects the fact that teachers adapt the curriculum to their assessment of each group's capacity to cope with the material. This adaptation occurs largely within the limits of difficulty set by the number of words available in the curriculum; that is, within district-wide definitions—commitments—of what should be accomplished in reading over the course of a year. Other organizational properties, the size of the group and its diversity, have little or no bearing on coverage.

The results from the regression analysis indicate that although the ability level of groups sets limits on what is covered, an equal or greater influence is exerted by conditions pertaining to curricular commitments. Whoever determines the curriculum exerts marked control over what is taught and, to a substantial extent, how much is taught. This influence when established at the district level must have two essential characteristics to be effective. First, it must represent defensible work that is appropriate for students and be assigned with sufficient time for its accomplishment. Second, since the influence is not a direct one, the support and competency of principals and teachers is essential for its realization.

We have argued that the curriculum is a driving force in school system organization. This means that in selecting curricular materials school systems acquire a basic component of their operating technology and enjoin its use. The technology operates through time at the classroom and group levels of organization. It entails the creation of social units for instruction (individuals, groups, whole classes) as well as the performance of instructional activities—conveying curricular knowledge to those units over time. As an organizational phenomenon, then, the curriculum represents both the school system's obligation to convey knowledge acceptable to the community and an element in the technology of classroom instruction. Through the activities of the organization, the former is transformed into the latter.

Acknowledgments

We thank Charles E. Bidwell, Adam Gamoran, Larry V. Hedges, Morris Janowitz, and David E. Wiley who made extremely helpful comments.

Appendix Correlation Matrix

	1	2	3	4	5	6	7
1 Coverage							
2 Materials—words	.59						
3 Length of school day	.65	.90					
4 Reading + L.A. time	.51	.78	.70				
5 Basal supervised time	.70	.45	.59	.60			
6 Group mean apt.	.72	.41	.33	.23	.20		
7 Group SD apt.	.48	.11	.10	.07	.27	.56	
8 Group size	.25	− .17	− .04	− .05	.30	.19	− .37

	Mean	SD
1	380.82	226.26
2	536.82	121.78
3	309.85	13.89
4	143.61	25.07
5	15.65	8.70
6	21.64	10.90
7	5.23	3.48
8	6.30	2.72

REFERENCES

Alexander, Karl L. and Cook, Martha. 1982. "Curricula and coursework: a surprise ending to a familiar story." *American Sociological Review* 47:626–640.

Apple, Michael W. 1979. *Ideology and Curriculum*, London: Routledge and Kegan Paul.

Apple, Michael W. (ed.). 1982. *Cultural and Economic Reproduction in Education*. London: Routledge and Kegan Paul.

The Bank Street Reading Series. 1966. New York: Macmillan.

Barr, Rebecca. 1985a. "Content coverage in classrooms." Pp. 985–989 in T. Husen and T. N. Postlethwait (eds.), *International Encyclopedia of Education*. Oxford: Pergamon.

Barr, Rebecca. 1985b. "A sociological analysis of the influence of class conditions on mathematics instruction." Paper presented at the annual meeting of the American Educational Research Association, Chicago.

Barr, Rebecca and Dreeben, Robert. 1983. *How Schools Work*. Chicago: University of Chicago Press.

Carnoy, Martin and Levin, Henry M. 1985. *Schooling and Work in the Democratic State*. Stanford, CA: Stanford University Press.

Chicago Mastery Learning Reading. 1981. Watertown, MA: Mastery Education Corp.

Comber, L. C. and Keeves, J. P. 1973. *Science Education in Nineteen Countries.* New York: Wiley.

Dreeben, Robert and Gamoran, Adam. 1986. "Race, instruction, and learning." *American Sociological Review* 51: in press.

Easton, David and Jack Dennis. 1969. *Children in the Political System.* New York: McGraw-Hill.

HBJ Bookmark Reading Program. 1979. New York: Harcourt, Brace, Jovanovich.

The Houghton Mifflin Readers. 1971. Boston: Houghton Mifflin.

Houghton Mifflin Reading Series. 1976. Boston: Houghton Mifflin.

Husen, Torsten. 1967. *International Study of Achievement in Mathematics.* New York: Wiley.

Janowitz, Morris. 1983. *The Reconstruction of Patriotism.* Chicago: University of Chicago Press.

Jennings, M. Kent and Richard G. Niemi. 1974. *The Political Character of Adolescence.* Princeton: Princeton University Press.

Merriam, Charles E. 1931. *The Making of Citizens.* Chicago: University of Chicago Press.

Meyer, John W. 1977. "Education as an institution." *American Journal of Sociology* 83:55–77.

Reading 720: Rainbow Edition. 1979. Lexington, MA: Ginn.

Torney, Judith V., Abraham N. Oppenheim, and Russell F. Farnen. 1975. *Civic Education in Ten Countries.* New York: Wiley.

Young, Michael F. D. (ed.). 1971. *Knowledge and Control.* London: Collier-Macmillan.

CHAPTER 3

Ability Grouping and Student Learning

MAUREEN T. HALLINAN

Grouping students by ability for instruction is a common pedagogical practice. In elementary schools it appears most frequently in the form of within-class ability grouping, that is, the
assignment of students in a class to instructional groups based
on their ability or achievement. In secondary schools it generally occurs in the form of tracking, or the assignment of students to different classes at the same grade level on the basis
of their ability.

The focus of this paper is within-class ability grouping,
although many of the arguments made are applicable to tracking as well. The main rationale for the practice of within-class
ability grouping is to permit teachers to gear instruction to the
aptitude and readiness of the students. It is believed that students will learn more if the level and pace of instruction matches

Maureen T. Hallinan • Department of Sociology, University of Notre Dame,
Notre Dame, IN 46556. The author gratefully acknowledges support for this
research from the National Institute of Education (NIE-G-81-009) through the
Wisconsin Center for Education Research.

their learning abilities. A secondary motivation for ability grouping is to assist teachers with the management and discipline of students. It is easier to obtain and hold the attention of a small group of students than a larger group.

Social science research on ability grouping has been concerned with three main questions: first, what are the consequences of ability grouping for student achievement; second, what are the factors that influence the formation and stability of ability groups; and third, are there social consequences for students of ability grouping?

Despite the rationale for its practice, empirical research is fairly consistent in showing that ability grouping has no main effect on student learning compared to whole-class instruction. However, ability grouping does differentially affect the achievement of students assigned to high and low groups. Comprehensive reviews of research on the effects of ability grouping (Brophy and Good, 1974; Good and Marshall, 1984) conclude that although ability grouping is sometimes beneficial to students of high ability, it generally impedes the academic progress of students in low groups. An implication of the differential effect of ability grouping on slow students is that grouping widens the class distribution of achievement, creating greater inequality between the students at the ends of the distribution. Further, the size of an ability group has been found to influence student achievement at all levels of ability. In a sample of 34 classes grouped by ability for reading, Hallinan and Sørensen (1985) showed that class size had no direct effect on reading achievement but that the larger the ability group, the slower the group members' progress in reading.

Recently, research has focused on factors influencing the formation of within-class ability groups and the process of assigning students to groups. Hallinan and Sørensen (1983) examined the number and size of reading and mathematics ability groups in several fourth-grade through seventh-grade classes. They found that teachers tended to form three ability groups of fairly equal size, regardless of the achievement distribution of the class, and that these groups remained stable over the school year. Some variation in ability group size was observed, however, in desegregated classes. Sørensen and Hallinan (1984) showed that the high-ability groups in desegregated classes were larger than those in all-black or all-white classes. In eight of the nine first-grade classes studied by Barr and Dreeben (1983), the teacher formed three ability groups. The size of the groups varied with the number of low-ability children in the class; a small number of low-ability students was associated with a small low-ability group.

Finally, ability grouping has been related to children's social relations. Hallinan and Sørensen (1985) found that same-race friendships were more likely to develop between students assigned to the same ability group than between those in different groups. Hallinan and Teixeira (1987) observed the same effect of assignment to the same ability group on cross-race friendships.

The growing body of literature on ability grouping firmly establishes its importance as a pedagogical practice in elementary schools. However, this research is concerned primarily with the determinants and consequences of ability grouping for children's cognitive and social development. What is conspicuously absent from these studies is a systematic investigation of the mechanisms that link ability grouping to educational outcome. Although we know that ability grouping differentially affects the achievement of bright and slow students, we do not know why or how this occurs. The instructional, cognitive, and social psychological processes that take place within ability groups and that affect student achievement have not been adequately specified. The mechanisms that transmit the effects of ability grouping on achievement are believed to occur through instruction as well as in response to structural and organizational factors in the classroom. The aim of this chapter is to identify characteristics of the learning process that are influenced by ability grouping and that mediate its effects on student achievement.

The next section will outline a general model of learning as it takes place in a school setting. The following section will show how the learning process is influenced by the practice of within-class ability grouping.

A MODEL OF LEARNING

Learning is a complex phenomenon characterized by the acquisition of knowledge, understanding, and skills. In a school setting, the material to be learned and skills to be acquired are generally defined by a curriculum. Mastery of the curriculum is measured by academic achievement tests and is a prerequisite for advancement to the next curriculum.

Several theories of learning are found in the literature. Classical learning theorists have concentrated on sequencing in the presentation of material (Hilgard and Bower, 1966), on imitation (Bandura, 1975), and on contingency and reinforcement (Miller and Dollard, 1941). Educational psychologists have focused on individual difference in learning (Bloom, 1976; Carroll, 1963). The sociological literature has been concerned with what characteristics of schools influence student achievement, aspirations, and future occupations. (For a summary of the school effects literature, see Spady, 1973).

The learning model to be discussed here is an extension of a sociological model originally outlined by Sørensen and Hallinan (1977). Although this particular model lies within the school effects tradition, its concern with the dynamics of learning also relates it to more social psychological formulations of the learning process. The Sørensen–Hallinan model conceptualizes student learning as a function of opportunities for learning and student aptitude and effort. Unlike traditional models, which express level of achievement as an additive function of individual and school characteristics, this model specifies change in achievement as an additive function of opportunities for learning and the ability and effort of a student. The functional form of the model is

$$d(y)/dt = s + by(t)$$

where $d(y)/dt$ is the rate of learning, s is a combined measure of aptitude and effort, b is a measure of opportunities for learning and $y(t)$ is the level of achievement at time t.

In this model, the concept of opportunities for learning is broadly defined and includes environmental as well as instructional factors. Moreover, ability and effort are treated as a single variable. In the present extension of the model, the notion of opportunities for learning is limited to characteristics of instruction and a conceptually distinct variable, the learning climate or environment, is added to the model. In addition, student ability and effort will be separated, with ability being conceptualized as an exogenous variable and motivation and effort as being endogenous to the system. These variables and their predicted interrelationships are presented in Figure 1.

Opportunities for learning, in this model, are seen as being provided through the instructional process. The learning climate is determined by teacher expectations and peer influences. These two variables, opportunity and climate, have an indirect effect on student learning, mediated by student motivation and effort. Motivation is causally prior to effort. Student aptitude is a function of intelligence and prior learning or readiness; like opportunities and climate, it has an indirect effect on learning that operates through the mediation of motivation and effort.

Opportunities for Learning

Opportunities for learning are presented to students through the instructional process. Instruction in schools is generally provided by a teacher who is sometimes assisted by teacher aides or peer tutors. It has two dimensions: quantity and quality. The former determines how much of the curriculum a student is exposed to; the latter influences how much of this material is actually learned.

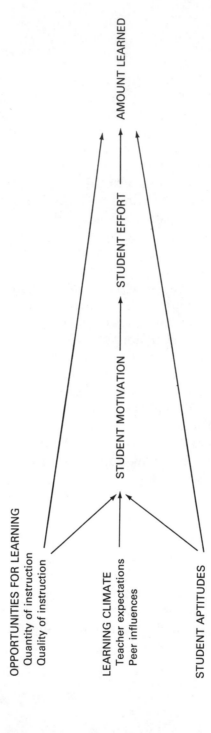

Figure 1. A model of student learning.

A simple argument relates quantity of instruction to learning. Students can learn only what they are exposed to. The amount of time actually spent learning, or time on task, is generally only some fraction of instructional time since it is influenced by other factors as well. Quality of instruction and student aptitude, motivation, and effort create the difference between instructional time or quantity of instruction and learning time.

A number of theoretical statements elaborate the relationship between quantity of instruction and learning (Carroll, 1963; Wiley and Harnischfeger, 1974; Fisher *et al.*, 1978). In his model of school learning, Carroll (1963) depicts learning as a function of aptitude, ability to understand instruction, quality of instruction, time allowed (quantity of instruction), and perseverance. Wiley and Harnischfeger (1974) posit that the amount of time actually spent learning is associated with pupil characteristics and with exposure to instruction (quantity of instruction). In the Beginning Teacher Evaluation Study (Fisher *et al.*, 1978), academic learning time is related to allotted time (quantity of instruction), engaged time, error rate, and relevance to a content domain.

Each of these theories includes amount or quantity of instruction or time allocated to instruction as a major determinant of learning. Yet, empirical support for the predicted positive relationship between quantity of instruction and student learning is not impressive. For example, whereas Wiley (1976) found that total number of hours in school has a strong positive effect on achievement in the EEO data, Karweit's (1976) analysis of this and other data sets showed only a modest to negligible effect of quantity of schooling on achievement.

The failure of empirical research to reveal a consistent positive effect of quantity of schooling on achievement may be due, in part, to the methodological limitations of the studies. The measures of quantity of schooling generally used are only gross indicators of instructional time. For example, the variable, number of hours in school, does not reflect how much of that time is devoted to non-instructional tasks. Moreover, the models are typically misspecified. The theoretical models of the learning process all imply interactions between instructional time and other aspects of the instructional process. Yet the empirical analyses generally portray instructional time only as a main effect.

In the model outlined here, quantity of instruction is depicted as having an indirect effect on learning, mediated by student motivation and effort. It interacts with all the other exogenous variables in the model. Increasing the quantity of instruction benefits learning only when the quality of instruction is satisfactory. A lengthy lesson that confuses students may produce less learning than a short well-presented lesson. Moreover, the aptitude of a student must be considered. A thirty-minute lesson is likely to be more fully comprehended by a high-ability student than by one of lower ability. The learning climate also influences the amount of instructional time during which the students actually attend to a lesson. A distracting learning climate decreases the proportion of instructional time during which a student is engaged in learning. Finally, students must be motivated and make an effort to learn through listening, concentrating and practicing before learning can take place. If a student is inattentive, the duration of the lesson is irrelevant to the learning process. An appropriate conceptualization of the learning process, then, relates quantity of instruction to other opportunities for learning, to the context of instruction and to student aptitude, motivation, and effort. Quantity of instruction, then, does not have only an additive effect on learning; it interacts with quality of instruction, learning climate, and student characteristics to affect time on task which, in turn, produces learning.

The second dimension of opportunities for learning is the quality of instruction. An examination of what are believed to be the central elements of the learning process is part of the process–product tradition of research (e.g. Dunkin and Biddle, 1974; Gage, 1972) which focuses on how teachers teach and what outcomes are produced in students by instruction. This tradition has produced useful lists or categorization schemes that disaggregate teaching and identify its component parts. Yet, these studies generally do not explicate the process that links teaching activities to learning. As Barr and Dreeben (1983) argue, the process–product research fails to establish why any particular teaching activity should be related to any given learning outcome.

Rather than examining these extensive lists of teaching activities, the focus here will be on the three elements of teaching believed to have the greatest influence on students' cognitive development. These are content, pacing, and method of presentation. Quality of instruction is seen to be determined primarily by these three components of instruction.

The content of instruction, generally defined by a school curriculum, is the information, knowledge, and skills that are to be learned by the students. It is presented through instructional materials, such as books and equipment, and through teacher explanations in the form of lectures, instructions, and demonstrations. A key characteristic of instruction, if it is to be of high quality, is that its content must be congruent with the aptitudes or level of comprehension of the students. Material that is too advanced for students to understand or too simple to engage their interests will not motivate the students to expend the effort needed to learn. The second component of instruction, pacing, is the rate at which the content of instruction is presented to students. Again, pace must be geared to the learning rate of students in order for them to understand the material and remain motivated to learn. Too fast or too slow a pace results in student discouragement or boredom and in their disengagement from the learning process.

Finally, method of instruction is the way in which a teacher presents the content of the curriculum to students. Instructional methods have been defined in several ways. For example, Lewin, Lippitt, and White (1939) describe teaching methods as authoritarian, democratic, or laissez-faire. Other schemes include teacher-directed instruction versus teacher–student interaction

(Flanders, 1965) or teacher instruction versus peer tutoring (Stodolsky, 1984). Still other schemes focus on the use of supplementary materials in instruction or the type of reward system (e.g. cooperative or competitive) that teachers use to motivate the students to learn (e.g., Slavin, 1977).

No clear guidance emerges from the research on teacher effectiveness that suggests which teaching method is superior and under what conditions. Yet a belief persists that different students learn more efficiently under different methods of instruction (Beckerman and Good, 1981) and occasionally research experiments bear this out (e.g., Anderson, Evertson, and Brophy, 1979; Evertson, 1982). What is obvious is that any method of instruction must be clear, well organized, and interesting in order to sustain student attention and produce learning. In addition, it can be argued that an instructional method is successful when it actively involves the students in the lesson. Any method that sustains student interest and involvement in the curriculum is likely to produce learning.

Climate of Instruction

Two dimensions of the learning climate or context of instruction that are critical to the learning process are teacher expectations for student performance and peer influences. Despite the methodological criticisms (Cooper and Tom, 1984) leveled against the early classical work on the effects of teacher expectations on student academic performance (Rosenthal and Jacobson, 1968), more recent and better designed research supports the same conclusion, namely, that the higher a teacher's expectations for a student, the better the student's performance. Conversely, the lower the teacher's expectations, the poorer the student's performance. This holds true regardless of the accuracy of the teacher's perceptions of the student's abilities.

Two mechanisms appear to link teacher expectations to student performance. First, teachers adapt the quantity and quality of instruction to their perceptions of student capabilities.

When teachers believe that students have high ability, they tend to stimulate and challenge them. Since they expect these students to be motivated, they may be less likely to perceive them as causing disciplinary problems. As a result, the teacher can spend more time with these students in instruction. Further, teachers tend to involve high-ability students more in the instructional process through question–answer, discussion, and so on. This leads to greater student attention and interest and consequently greater effort to learn. In contrast, if teachers have low expectations of student performance, they are apt to simplify instruction by limiting the content and slowing the pace. They expect and therefore see more disciplinary problems and deal with these at a loss to instructional time.

The second way teachers' expectations influence student performance is through their effect on students' self-confidence or self-image as learners. As Mead (1934) points out, one's self-image is formed through interaction with others. When students discover that a significant other, such as a teacher, believes that they are capable of difficult work, they begin to believe it of themselves. Similarly, when a teacher communicates low expectations for pupils, it is likely to diminish the students' opinions of their own capabilities. Self-image, in turn, affects motivation and effort. The higher a student's self-confidence, the greater the effort the student generally will expend in the learning process. Pupils with little self-confidence are less likely to study hard, believing that they have little control over the outcome of their efforts. Consequently, teacher expectations affect student performance by influencing student opportunities for learning and by affecting their motivation to learn.

A second aspect of the learning climate is peer influences. It is a well-documented finding in the social science literature that peers affect a student's attitudes and behaviors. In particular, a large number of empirical studies show that the value climate of a school or classroom affects a student's academic achievement and educational aspirations (see Spady, 1973, for a review of some of these studies), and other studies reveal peer influences on social behavior (Coleman, 1961; Cusick, 1973;

Newcomb, 1961). The most common theoretical explanations of peer influences are normative and comparative reference group theory (Kelley, 1947; Kemper, 1968), role modeling (Bandura and Walters, 1963; Miller and Dollard, 1941), and labeling (Goffman, 1961; Tannenbaun, 1938). Peers are believed to communicate norms and standards for behavior through interaction in a group which also provides a basis for comparison and evaluation of the student's own behavior. In addition, peers shape a pupil's attitudes and behavior by serving as models for imitation and by exerting pressure on an individual to adhere to the behavioral expectations of a label. In attempting to meet these expectations, a student's attitudes and behavior tend to change in the directions of conformity with their peers.

Of concern here are the consequences of peer influences on student attitudes and behavior for student motivation and effort. Students having peers who value academic achievement or are serious about learning are more likely to be motivated to learn themselves. However, students whose peers devalue learning or who place negative labels on those students who are involved in the learning process are likely to expend less effort on learning out of fear of sanction or rejection. Thus peers are an important component of the learning climate of a classroom or group and exert a positive or negative influence, or possibly both, on a student's motivation to study and effort to learn.

Student Aptitude

The amount of material a student learns, other things being equal, is a function of the student's aptitudes or ability to learn. Aptitude is determined, in part, by a student's intelligence, which is measured, more or less accurately, by an IQ test. Aptitude is also affected by background factors, such as social class, home environment, number of siblings, which affect a student's readiness to learn. Variation in student motivation, effort, and achievement is caused in part by differences in student aptitudes. The easier a student finds learning, the more readily the student will be engaged in the learning process. In addition, differences in aptitude explain variation in the way students take advantage of the opportunities for learning provided through instruction and in the way students are influenced by their learning climate.

Student Motivation and Effort

Student motivation refers to how much a student wants to learn. It is elicited by competitive, cooperative, or individualistic goals (Ames and Ames, 1984) and varies with student characteristics and environmental conditions. Specifically, opportunities for learning, the learning climate, and student aptitude have direct effects on student motivation. Student effort is how hard a student tries to learn. Effort has two dimensions, length and intensity. It is sometimes referred to as perseverance, or time on task, reflecting the time dimension of the concept. Effort is directly related to student motivation. It is an indirect function of the cognitive and psychological characteristics of students such as student aptitude, need for achievement, curiosity, educational or career aspirations, and sense of control over one's environment. Student effort is related to opportunities for learning as provided by the instructional process and to the learning climate through the mediation of motivation.

ABILITY GROUPING AND STUDENT LEARNING

This section will analyze how the learning process, as described in the model outlined above, is affected by the pedagogical practice of ability grouping. It will be argued that ability grouping influences the opportunities for learning that are presented to students in the form of the quantity and quality of instruction, that it creates a specific learning climate within each ability group by affecting teacher expectations and peer influences, and that it modifies student aptitudes and readiness for learning. These determinants of learning—opportunities, climate, and student aptitudes—affect student motivation and effort, which produce learning. The effect of ability grouping on learning, then, occurs primarily through its influence on the exogenous factors depicted in the learning model.

Ability Grouping and Opportunities for Learning

Ability grouping affects the quantity or amount of instruction a student receives from the teacher in a number of ways. Whether or not a teacher organizes students into ability groups for instruction in a particular subject, such as reading, generally does not affect the total amount of instructional time allocated to that subject. In ability-grouped classes the instructional time given to reading is divided up, evenly or unevenly, across the different ability groups. Consequently, the amount of time ability-grouped students spend in instruction with the teacher is necessarily less than it would be with whole-class instruction. Other things being equal, this represents a disadvantage of ability grouping, if a positive relationship does indeed exist between quantity of instruction and achievement.

On the other hand, the quality of instruction is believed to be higher in ability groups than it is when the whole class is taught together because the lessons can be geared to the students' aptitudes and because each student receives more individual attention during instruction. To the extent that this is true, the improved quality of instruction in ability groups may compensate for the reduction in instructional time resulting from grouping. If the quality of instruction in ability groups is not superior to that in whole-class instruction, then it is difficult to see how ability grouping can be justified as a pedagogical device in light of its reduction in the quantity of instruction students receive.

Another way in which ability grouping affects quantity of instruction is through a teacher's allocation of instructional time across groups. Norms governing the equal treatment of students in the classroom lead many teachers to distribute their time equally across ability groups. Moreover, structural or organizational features of the classroom, including scheduling considerations and space factors, may necessitate instructional periods of the same length for each group. As a result, all ability-grouped students in a particular classroom may receive the same amount of instruction from the teacher. However, students have different learning needs and require different amounts of instructional time to learn the same material. The equal allocation of teacher time across ability groups does not accommodate individual differences in learning rates. On the contrary, it disadvantages slow students because they have less instructional time relative to the amount of time they need to learn than do high-ability students. Although the quality of whole-class instruction may not be as high as ability-grouped instruction, it does provide more teacher time for students and this may be more critical for slow students than for brighter ones.

Furthermore, the assumption underlying the equal distribution of teacher time across ability groups seems to be that the amount of time allocated for instruction is the same as the amount of time actually spent in instruction. This is likely not the case. Students in low-ability groups may require more time for organization and discipline than students in higher-ability groups. They are also likely to perform academic tasks, such as reading, more slowly than their brighter peers. These factors reduce the amount of instruction that the teacher can provide in low-ability groups, resulting in the students' receiving a smaller quantity of instruction than their peers in a high-ability group.

If teachers do not adhere to a norm of equal instructional time for all students, they are apt to spend more time with the low-ability students than those of higher ability because the former are seen as being less self-directed and more dependent on teacher input. The actual amount of instruction may effectively be the same across groups, of course, if the teacher spends more time on administrative matters and discipline in the low-ability groups than in the higher ones. But if the slower students do actually receive longer instruction, they are likely to learn more. There seems to be little rationale for a teacher's providing less instructional time for the low-ability group than for higher groups even if the low group is small since slow students need more time to learn and are more dependent on teacher instruction. In short, from the point of view of quantity of instruction, students in a low-ability group are disadvantaged compared to their peers in higher groups unless a teacher provides a longer period of instruction for them.

Pace of instruction is also related to the quantity of instruction received. One reason for ability grouping is to adjust the pace of instruction to students' learning needs. The pace of instruction is faster in high-ability groups than in low groups because the brighter students learn more quickly. If the amount of time allocated to instruction is the same for all groups, the high-ability students will be exposed to more material than the low-ability students. Again, longer instructional time is needed for the slow students if they are to cover the same amount of material as their brighter peers.

Another factor influencing the quantity of instruction received in ability groups is the number and size of the groups. If groups are unequal in size but are instructed for the same length of time, then the students in the small groups will receive more instruction, in the sense of individual attention from the teacher, than those in the larger groups. In addition, smaller groups require less time for organization and discipline, which leaves more time for instruction. On the other hand, the large number of students doing unsupervised work while the teacher is instructing a small group may cause teachers to interrupt their lessons to monitor these students' behavior, thus reducing instructional time. This problem is reduced if a teacher aide is available to supervise the students who are not working directly with the teacher. If instructional time is distributed unequally across unequal-sized groups, the quantity of instruction and the amount of individual attention a student receives from the teacher depend on the size of the group and the length of the instructional period. Teacher decisions in this regard could result in a situation that is quite equitable in terms of the amount of direct instruction each student receives or one in which large discrepancies exist from one student to another. Finally, if teachers divide students equally across groups and provide the same amount of instruction in each group, then the more groups that are formed, the less instruction each student will receive. Nevertheless, an advantage of small groups is that they tend to be more homogeneous than larger groups which facilitates gearing instruction to the students' level. This should result in better though less instruction.

In an ability-grouped class, when the teacher is working with one group of students, the other students are usually assigned seatwork, which is generally unsupervised or supervised only by a teacher aide. The usefulness of seatwork for student learning is questionable. Students often find it boring, resulting in their expending little effort on this work. Teachers are necessarily less attuned to the quality of the students' seatwork and to the difficulties they may be having with the assignment because they are engaged in teaching another ability group. As a result, students are likely not to receive help or have errors corrected until later, if at all. This, too, leads to student discouragement and distraction or misbehavior. In general, seatwork, or other unsupervised tasks assigned to students, is seen at best to be less effective than direct teacher instruction and at worst to be fairly useless. This represents a negative consequence of ability grouping for student learning.

The small benefit of seatwork that may exist for students varies with student ability and aptitude. Brighter students are more capable of remaining on task when unsupervised than slow students who need more direction and assistance. Consequently, seatwork would appear to be less effective for students in low-ability groups than for those in high groups. In classes wherein teachers allow more instructional time for the low-ability group than for the other groups, this has the added advantage for the slow students of reducing the time they must spend on seatwork.

The quality of instruction as well as the quantity differs

across ability groups. We focused earlier on content, pace, and method of instruction as critical components of the quality of instruction. Ability grouping affects each of these components. The content of a curriculum is presented to students through teacher instruction as well as through basic textbooks, skill packages, workbooks, and the like. The choice of these materials is generally made at the school district level rather than being left to the discretion of the teacher. The students in the class usually are expected to start at the beginning of a series in, say, reading or mathematics and progress to a certain point in order to merit promotion to the next grade. The same basic core of material is expected to be covered in all the ability groups. Most students progress further than required and move on to more advanced books or work on supplementary material while a few may not complete or master the required material and are retained at the same grade level for another year.

When students are grouped by ability, they cover the curriculum material at different rates. The difference, then, in content coverage across ability groups is related to the pace of instruction. The high-ability groups who are taught at a faster pace are exposed to more materials than the low-ability groups. Another difference between content coverage in high and low groups lies in the supplementary materials a teacher provides for the students. These are not usually dictated by the curriculum and provide opportunities for teachers to be creative in preparing work for their students. It is likely, however, that since the first responsibility of teachers is to cover the curriculum, they will insist that students who progress slowly work primarily on the required materials while giving the faster students the supplementary materials. Often these assignments are more interesting than the required curriculum materials. Moreover, they provide variety in the learning experience which helps avoid student boredom and loss of motivation and effort.

Methods of instruction also differ across ability groups. It is generally believed that students who find learning difficult or whose comprehension level is low benefit more from repetition and rote learning than from other teaching techniques. Teachers seem to feel that the less they can appeal to a pupil's logic or understanding, the more they must rely on memorization as a learning device. A number of studies show that teachers use structured instructional methods disproportionately more in low-ability groups than in high groups. In an ethnographic study of teachers in grade classrooms, Stern and Shavelson (1981) showed that lesson plans for the low-ability group differed considerably from those for the high-ability group. With low-ability students teachers emphasized decoding and basic comprehension skills and gave highly structured assignments, whereas with high-ability groups they stressed flexibility in procedures and assignments and emphasis on sophisticated comprehension skills. Martin and Evertson (1980) showed that teachers used a more direct, less flexible approach with lower-ability students.

Differences in teaching methods across ability groups are significant only if one method is superior to another. The little research that exists on this topic appears to indicate that a particular method is effective to the extent that it sustains student interest. Rote learning and memorization, which are more prevalent in low-ability groups, are believed to be less interesting for students and less engaging than other types of instruction such as discussion, question and answer sessions, and so on. Indeed, Flanders (1965) argues that rote methods create dependency among students and are obstacles to the development of curiosity and initiative. Consequently, students in low-ability groups are likely to become more inattentive during instruction than those in high-ability groups because the methods of instruction employed are inherently less interesting. This represents an obstacle to learning for students in low-ability groups.

Quality of instruction, then, varies across ability groups through variation in the content, pace, and methods of instruction. In low-ability groups, less material is covered because the curriculum is presented at a slower pace and the methods of instruction are less interesting and challenging. Thus, the quality of instruction in low-ability groups is seen as being inferior to that in higher groups.

Ability Grouping and Learning Climate

Ability grouping has significant consequences for the two dimensions of the learning climate of concern here, namely, teacher expectations and peer influences. When teachers assign students to ability groups for instruction, they generally rely on one or more of the following criteria: standardized achievement tests, teacher-designed tests, teacher perceptions of student ability, motivation and maturity, and recommendations of other teachers who have already worked with the student. When objective measures of achievement are not available, as, for example, when students enter first grade, teacher perceptions of student ability must be relied on. When objective measures of achievement are available, teachers may use these test scores or they may emphasize other criteria for assignment such as behavioral characteristics and verbal fluency.

Regardless of the criteria used, the assignment of a student to a particular ability group reveals the teacher's expectations for that student's academic performance. Other teachers, parents, and the students themselves become aware of what these expectations are. The teacher subsequently adjusts the quantity and quality of instruction to the mean level of each ability group in response to his or her expectations for the achievement of the average student in the group.

The fact that ability groups tend to be stable over the school year suggests that little change occurs in teacher expectations over time. This is curious since it seems to ignore such commonly recognized occurrences as growth spurts or sudden changes in learning readiness, changes in student emotional or social development, and variation in home influences on student behavior. It appears that students rarely succeed in changing a teacher's perception of their ability to the extent that they are transferred to another group, either at a higher or lower ability level. It may be that when students are grouped, teachers focus more on group differences in performance than on individual differences and become less aware of individual deviations from the mean achievement of the group.

Teachers may overreact to the labels that are attached to ability groups and have lower expectations for the students in the low group and higher expectations for the students in the high group than are appropriate. This would be reflected in the way they instruct the different groups. Several studies reviewed by Brophy and Good (1974) show that this is the case. Students in low tracks were found to fall increasingly behind those of equal ability in higher tracks while pupils in high-ability groups achieved more than their peers of equal ability who were not in high groups. Teachers seemed to have higher expectations for students in high-ability groups than for students of the same ability who were not grouped for instruction. They minimized disciplinary problems and put greater effort into motivating students in the high-ability groups. In contrast, teachers praised students in low-ability groups more than students of the same ability who were not grouped, seeming to be satisfied with lesser accomplishments from students in the low groups.

Finally, teacher expectations constrain the learning of students who are initially placed incorrectly in an ability group. If some students are assigned to lower groups than is appropriate, they will be denied the opportunities to be exposed to material that they are capable of learning. Further, teachers will not expect them to achieve as much as they are capable of and will not challenge them to greater accomplishment. This process has a cumulative effect on student learning. The missed opportunities for learning will not be retrieved unless the student is advanced to a higher-ability group but this tends not to happen. Over time, then, pupils' achievement will likely regress toward the mean of the group in which they have been placed. The opposite, of course, occurs when students are placed in a higher group than their capabilities warrant. If the difference between the students' aptitudes and the level of instruction in the higher group is not so great as to discourage the students and weaken their self-confidence, then the greater opportunities for learning and the higher teacher expectations for students in the high groups should result in increased achievement for those students originally misassigned by the end of the school year.

Teacher expectations also affect a student's self-image. There are several ways in which teachers can communicate their expectations for student performance in ability groups. It can occur, for example, through the content, pace, and method of instruction, through the kinds of work rewarded and the nature of rewards, through discipline, and through comparisons with other groups. When students realize what a teacher's expectations are for their work, they are likely to produce that level of work, believing that the teacher's evaluation of their capabilities is valid. Their image of their own abilities is being shaped in part by the teacher's expectations. If a teacher's expectations are inappropriate, as happens, for example, when a student is assigned to the wrong group, then the student's self-image may be adversely affected, inflated or deflated by the teacher's assumption. Whether or not a grouping assignment is accurate, teacher expectations are a major influence on students' perceptions of their abilities and these, in turn, affect their motivation and effort to learn.

Peer influences on student learning also differ across ability groups. In high-ability groups a student is more apt to find peers who have positive attitudes toward learning and whose motivation to learn is strong. These students set norms for task involvement and act as learning models for their peers. Fewer learning models are likely to be available in low-ability groups where students find learning more difficult and less rewarding. Moreover, in low-ability groups peers are likely to set norms and standards endorsing behavior that detracts from learning. Eder (1981) showed that the inattentive behavior of first-grade students during reading instruction was considerably greater in low-ability groups than in high groups. The disengagement of some group members from the lesson tended to distract all the students in the group. In a study of twelve first-grade classes,

Gamoran (1984) controlled for differential instruction and found a small effect of level of group on student achievement which he attributed to the effect of peer influences. Moreover, students often engage in modeling and imitate their peers' disruptive behavior, which again weakens the learning climate. Even teacher efforts to redirect the students' attention to the lesson can distract the students, resulting in a less productive instructional period. Consequently, the learning climate in a low-ability group tends to be less conducive to student learning than the climate in a high group both because teacher expectations for student performance are lower, resulting in fewer opportunities for learning, and because peer influences are less supportive of academic behavior.

Ability Grouping and Student Aptitudes

Since aptitude is a function of student capability or readiness to learn as well as of intelligence, it is influenced by a student's prior learning history. For some students, ability grouping is part of that educational history. Ability grouping is seen here as determining the opportunities for learning that are provided to a student and creating the environment in which learning takes place. Since these opportunities and learning climates differ across ability groups, they have a differential impact on the amount a student learns during a school year. The more that is learned, the higher the student's aptitude or the better the student's preparation for learning the curriculum to be presented in the next grade. Ideally, ability grouping would maximize the learning of all students through instruction geared to their capabilities. In this case, differences in aptitude would not be attributable to ability grouping but rather to ability differences and socialization factors. But when ability grouping deprives some students of learning opportunities to which they are capable of responding and fails to help students achieve their learning potential, it has the effect of reducing their aptitudes and readiness for further learning. This effect is cumulative over time since the amount of learning that could have taken place but does not reduces a student's aptitude at each subsequent grade. On the other hand, when ability grouping stimulates students by providing learning challenges, it increases their aptitude in a way that will also be cumulative across grade.

Ability Grouping and Student Motivation and Effort

As seen above, ability grouping conditions the effects of opportunities for learning, the learning climate, and student aptitudes on student motivation, effort, and achievement. This makes the practice of ability grouping a powerful agent affecting the learning process. To the extent that ability grouping decreases the quantity and quality of instruction provided to a student, creates a less than optimal learning environment, and reduces student aptitudes, it lessens student motivation and effort to learn and consequently has a negative effect on student achievement. For those students, generally in high-ability groups, for whom ability grouping increases opportunities for learning, enhances the learning climate, and improves student aptitudes, ability grouping has a positive indirect effect on motivation and effort and therefore on student achievement.

CONCLUSIONS

This chapter specifies the mechanisms through which within-class ability grouping affects student learning and growth in academic achievement. A model of learning is presented that explains student learning in terms of the opportunities for learning that are provided to the student in the form of the quantity and quality of instruction, the climate or environment in which instruction takes place, and student aptitude, which is seen as being determined, at least in part, by a student's prior learning experiences. These three factors—opportunities for learning, learning climate, and student aptitude—have effects on student achievement that are primarily mediated by student motivation and effort.

The pedagogical practice of ability grouping is seen as affecting learning through its influence on the exogenous factors in the learning model. Ability grouping determines the quantity of instruction a student receives; it also influences the quality of instruction by affecting content, pace, and method. Grouping affects the climate of instruction through its association with teacher expectations for student performance and with peer influences in the form of pupil behavior during instruction and student norms about academic achievement. Finally, grouping affects student aptitudes by influencing prior learning and readiness for instruction.

The chapter argues that the differential impact of ability grouping on the achievement of students in high- and low-ability groups that is often documented in social science research can be explained in terms of the way in which ability grouping conditions the three major factors affecting learning. Opportunities for learning, instructional climate, and student aptitudes vary across ability groups and in general favor students in the high-ability group. When instructional groups meet for the same length of time, which is usually the case, students in the high group generally receive more instruction than those in the low group because they spend more time on task during instruction than do students in the low group. Quality of instruction in the high group tends to be better because methods of instruction and materials are more interesting. The climate is more conducive to learning in the high-ability group since teacher expectations are higher and peer influences more supportive of learning. The aptitude of students in the high group is maximized, producing greater readiness for the next curricular experience while the aptitude of students in the low group is diminished through a reduction in opportunities to learn.

The implications of this analysis are straightforward. Most of the factors identified herein as determinants of learning are amenable to teacher manipulation or intervention. Consequently, they can be modified within the structure of ability groups to provide greater equality of opportunities to learn for all students. Ability groups can be structured in such a way that the quantity of instruction provided in each group is responsive to student needs. This may require deviation from a norm of equal instructional time by increasing the length of instruction for the low-ability group since these students require more time to learn than brighter students. Teachers can insure that the instructional methods and materials they use in the low-ability group are challenging and engaging. They can be aware of the sources of their expectations for pupil performance and readily adjust those expectations when new information about students becomes available. This would undoubtedly require greater flexibility in assigning students to ability groups and in moving students from one group to another during the school year. The problem of negative peer influences in the low-ability group could be dealt with by creating a smaller low-ability group or by carefully structuring the reward system in the group and in the classroom.

In short, this analysis of the mechanisms that transmit the effects of ability grouping to student learning reveals several ways in which teacher decisions and intervention could improve the learning of students assigned to the low-ability group. To the extent that this is done, ability grouping could become a useful technique for improving the learning of all students regardless of their position in the achievement distribution of the class.

REFERENCES

Ames, Carole and Russell Ames. 1984. "Systems of student and teacher motivation: toward a qualitative definition." *Journal of Educational Psychology* 76(4):535–556.

Anderson, Linda, Carolyn Evertson, and Jere Brophy. 1979. "An experimental study of effective teaching in first-grade reading groups." *Elementary School Journal* 79:193–223.

Bandura, Albert. 1977. *Social Learning Theory*. Morristown, NJ: General Learning Press.

Barr, Rebecca and Robert Dreeben. 1983. *How Schools Work*. Chicago: University of Chicago Press.

Beckerman, Terrill and Thomas Good. 1981. "The classroom ratio of high-and-low aptitude students and its effect on achievement." *American Educational Research Journal* 18:317–327.

Bloom, Benjamin S. 1976. *Human Characteristics and School Learning*. New York: McGraw-Hill.

Brophy, Jere and Thomas L. Good. 1974. *Teacher–Student Relationships: Causes and Consequences*. New York: Holt, Rinehart and Winston.

Carroll. 1963. "A model of school learning." *Teachers College Record* 64(8):723–733.

Coleman, James. 1961. *The Adolescent Society*. New York: Free Press.

Cooper, Harris and David Tom. 1984. "Teacher expectation research: a review with implications for classroom instruction." *Elementary School Journal* 85(1):77–89.

Cusick, Philip. 1973. *Inside High School*. New York: Holt, Rinehart and Winston.

Dunkin, Michael and Bruce Biddle. 1974. *The Study of Teaching*. New York: Holt, Rinehart and Winston.

Eder, Donna. 1981. "Ability grouping as a self-fulfilling prophecy: a microanalysis of teacher–student interaction." *Sociology of Education* 54(July): 151–162.

Evertson, Carolyn. 1982. "Differences in instructional activities in average- and low-achieving junior high English and math classes." *Elementary School Journal* 82:329–350.

Fisher, Charles, Nikola Filby, Richard Marliave, Leonard Cahen, Marilyn Dishaw, Jeffrey Moore, and David Berliner. 1978. *Teaching Behaviors, Academic Learning Time and Student Achievement*. Final Report of Phase III-B, Beginning Teacher Evaluation Study. Technical Report V-1. San Francisco: Far West Laboratory for Educational Research and Development.

Flanders, Ned. 1965. *Teacher Influence, Pupil Attitudes and Achievement*. Washington, D.C.: U.S. Department of Health, Education and Welfare Cooperative Research Monograph No. 12.

Gage, Nathaniel. 1972. *Teacher Effectiveness and Teacher Education*. Palo Alto, CA: Pacific.

Gamoran, Adam. 1984. "Instructional, institutional and social effects of ability grouping." Unpublished manuscript. University of Wisconsin.

Goffman, Erving. 1961. *Asylums*. Garden City, NY: Doubleday Anchor.

Good, Thomas and Susan Marshall. 1984. "Do students learn more in heterogeneous or homogeneous groups?" Pp 15–51 in Penelope Peterson, Louise Cherry Wilkinson, and Maureen T. Hallinan (eds.), *The Social Context of Instruction*. San Diego: Academic Press.

Hallinan, Maureen T. and Aage B. Sørensen. 1985. Class size, ability group size and student achievement. *American Journal of Education* 94, 1:71–89.

Hallinan, Maureen T. and Aage B. Sørensen. 1983. "The formation and stability of ability groups." *American Sociological Review* 48(6):838–851.

Hallinan, Maureen T. and Ray Teixeira. 1987. "Students' interracial friendships: individual characteristics, structural effects and racial differences. *American Journal of Education* 95(4).

Hilgard, Ernest and Gordon Bower. 1966. *Theories of Learning.* New York: Appleton-Century-Crofts.

Karweit, Nancy. 1976. "Quality of schooling: a major educational factor?" *Educational Researcher* 5(2):15–17.

Kelley, Harold H. 1947. "Two functions of reference groups." Pp. 410–414 in Swanson, Newcomb, and Hartley (eds.), *Readings in Social Psychology.* New York: Holt, Rinehart and Winston.

Kemper, Theodore. 1968. "Reference groups, socialization and achievement." *American Sociological Review* 33:31–45.

Lewin, Kurt, Ronald Lippitt, and Ralph White. 1939. "Patterns of aggressive behavior in experimentally created social climates." *Journal of Social Psychology* 1:271–279.

Martin, John and Carolyn Evertson. 1980. *Teachers' Interactions with Reading Groups of Differing Ability Levels.* Technical Report No. R-4093. Austin: University of Texas, Research and Development Center for Teacher Education.

Mead, George H. 1934. *Mind, Self and Society.* Chicago: University of Chicago Press.

Miller, Neal and John Dollard. 1941. *Social Learning and Imitation.* New Haven, CN: Yale University Press.

Newcomb, Theodore. 1961. *The Acquaintance Process.* New York: Holt, Rinehart and Winston.

Rosenthal, Robert and Lenore Jacobson. 1968. *Pygmalion in the Classroom: Teacher Expectation and Pupils' Intellectual Development.* New York: Holt, Rinehart and Winston.

Slavin, Robert E. 1977. "Classroom reward structure: an analytical and practical review." *Review of Educational Research* 47(4):633–650.

Sørensen, Aage B. and Maureen T. Hallinan. 1977. "A reconceptualization of school effects." *Sociology of Education* 50(4):273–289.

Sørensen, Aage B. and Maureen T. Hallinan. 1984. "Race effects on assignment to ability groups." Pp. 85–103 in Peterson, Wilkinson, and Maureen T. Hallinan (eds.), *The Social Context of Instruction.* San Diego: Academic Press.

Spady, William G. 1973. "The impact of school resources on students." Pp. 135–177 in Kerlinger (ed.), *Review of Research in Education.* Itasca, IL: F. E. Peacock.

Stern, Paula and Richard Shavelson. 1981. "The relationship between teachers' grouping decisions and instructional beahviors: an ethnographic study of reading instruction." Paper presented at the meetings of the American Educational Research Association, Los Angeles.

Stodolsky, Susan. 1984. "Frameworks for studying instructional processes in peer work-groups." Pp. 107–124 in Penelope Peterson, Louise Cherry Wilkinson, and Maureen T. Hallinan (eds.), *The Social Context of Instruction*. San Diego: Academic Press.

Tannenbaum, Frank. 1938. *Crime and Community*. Boston: Ginn.

Wiley, David. 1976. "Another hour, another day: quantity of schooling, a potent path for policy." Pp. 225–265 in Sewell, Robert M. Hauser, and David L. Featherman (eds.), *Schooling and Achievement in American Society*. New York: Academic Press.

Wiley, David and Annegret Harnischfeger. 1974. "Explosion of a myth: quantity of schooling and exposure to instruction, major educational vehicles." *Educational Researcher* 3(4):7–12.

CHAPTER 4

Diversity, Equity, and Classroom Processes

NANCY KARWEIT

INTRODUCTION

Providing education for all citizens and maintaining high educational standards are basic goals of the American educational system. The tension between providing equity of opportunity and excellence in service has long been recognized. In its current version, this tension between excellence and equity has become highlighted as schools wrestle with the issue of raising standards on the one hand while maintaining minimum competencies on the other.

The tension between standards and equity is rarely discussed at the level of classroom practice although classrooms must surely be critical junctures for understanding the operation and consequences of assumptions and beliefs about equity, diversity, and excellence. For it is in the day-to-day activities within classrooms that the tensions between equity and standards are resolved. Although many decisions are made outside

Nancy Karweit • The Johns Hopkins University Center for Social Organization of Schools, Baltimore, MD 21218.

the classroom door, their impact and their ultimate effectiveness depend largely upon what transpires within the classroom. Learning and instruction are the major goals of schools; classrooms are the major settings wherein these goals are addressed. How classroom teachers cope with issues of equity, standards, and student differences, then, is an important, if not the most important, element in how schools actually function to provide or restrict opportunities for student success. The significance of teachers as enactors of societal as well as their own views of equitable treatment is especially high in elementary schools where students spend almost the entire day with the same teacher.

This chapter discusses the major ways of arranging instruction in groups in light of these concerns about standards and equity. It is primarily addressed to elementary school instruction. The methods of instruction considered are within-class grouping, whole-class instruction, individualized instruction, and mastery learning. Although not exhaustive, this list does comprise the major ways in which elementary instruction is presently carried out.

The basic question addressed here is the suitability of particular methods for attaining the twin goals of raising standards and maintaining minimum competencies. This question is addressed by a series of exercises in which different expectations for performance and resource levels are applied to a model of classroom learning.

Several key assumptions are made in carrying out these exercises:

1. It is possible to portray classroom processes by a model that includes student aptitude and effort, teacher effort, quality of instruction and time.
2. Classroom processes differ under different instructional methods.
3. Classroom average achievement outcomes are fairly similar across the different methods even though the processes are different.

The chapter begins by describing a model of instruction in classrooms. The model is an adaptation of Carroll's model of learning, which incorporates instructional grouping practices as a specific component. In the next section, a description of the processes by which different instructional methods operate is offered. Finally, an examination of how each method might be altered to raise standards and to attain minimum competencies is carried out.

A MODEL OF CLASSROOM LEARNING

Carroll's model of learning is the usual starting point for most discussions of learning in classrooms (Carroll, 1963). Carroll defined the degree of learning as the ratio of the time spent learning a topic to the time needed to learn a topic. In turn, time spent and time needed were defined as functions of individual and classroom-level characteristics, namely, allocated time, student effort, quality of instruction, and student aptitude and ability to benefit from the instruction.

Carroll's model was a major development in the conceptualization of individual learning as a function of the operation of individual and classroom factors. Nonetheless, because the model does not specifically incorporate the effects of instructional organizations and grouping arrangements, it is not completely suited for exploring how these manipulable features of classrooms influence student learning. In the next paragraphs, then, we present an adaptation of Carroll's model to include the effects of classroom organization on learning.

The amount of time a student spends learning is an important element in his eventual success or failure in school. Time spent is the result of many different factors including the management and scheduling skills of the teacher, the student's interest in the topic, and the appropriateness of the instructional material. These elements of adequate time, quality of instruction, and student effort must all be present for learning to occur. For example, if a teacher provides an excellent lesson to which a student pays minimal attention, little new learning will take place. Another way to state this is to say that the factors time, quality, and effort are multiplicatively related. For example, if a teacher has scheduled an hour for mathematics instruction and the instruction is appropriate for a student only 60 percent of that hour and the student pays attention 90 percent of this time, then the real amount of time spent will be 60 minutes × .60 × .90, or about 49 minutes.

Thus, in the view of learning in classrooms presented here we assume that time spent is the actual effective learning time, defined as the product of allocated time, attention rate, and appropriateness rate, or the product of time, effort, and quality.

Grouping practices have direct and indirect effects on these factors which define time spent and time needed. Figure 1 depicts these effects on the use of time, on the quality of instruction, and on the attention and effort made by students. This model implies, then, that the operation of classroom processes producing learning will be conditioned by the method of instructional organization. For example, time use patterns will

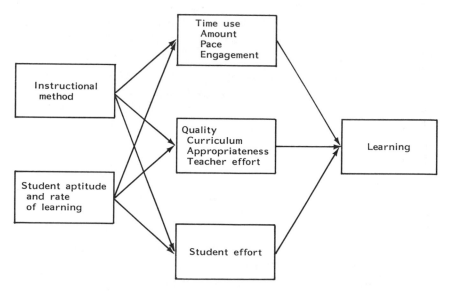

Figure 1. Effects of classroom organization on time spent and time needed

of necessity be different in whole-class and within-class grouping arrangements because of requirements of the method. The
next paragraphs detail how the particular grouping arrangements affect time, quality, and effort. Instructional method
affects the amount of instructional time, the pace of instructional events, and the engagement rate of students during
instruction. The amount of instructional time is the amount of
the allocated time actually used for instruction after time for
management, transitions, and disruptions is deducted. Practices that group and regroup students for instruction, such as
within-class grouping and individualization, will have lower
amounts of actual instructional time than whole-class methods
because of the management time needed to accomplish the
method. We expect that on average whole-class methods will
be able to utilize a greater fraction of allocated instructional
time for instruction than will within-class grouping, mastery
learning, or individualized methods.

The second time variable of interest is the pace of instruction. How teachers decide to pace instruction to a group of
diverse students is not entirely understood, but available evidence suggests the existence of a phenomenon called "the steering group" that guides teacher practice. Dahloff (1971) coined
this phrase, the steering group, to describe the teacher practice
of gearing instruction to that group of students at about the
average or slightly below average achievement level. According
to this view, teachers check for comprehension and understanding with members of this group and decide whether to
go on, go over, or switch gears depending upon how the steering group responds.

Instructional grouping practices determine the ability composition of the instructional groups and, through the operation
of the steering group, the instructional pace. In turn, pace is a
major determinant of the content covered (Barr and Dreeben,
1983).

Student engagement is affected in several ways by instructional grouping arrangements. The lesson format, the ease of
supervising and monitoring student work, and the motivational

climate of the group affect student engagement. All these factors are directly affected by the organization of the classroom
for instruction.

Student engagement with learning appears to be highest
in settings in which there is a high continuity of behavior.
Kounin (1970) described this phenomenon as the "signal system
of the lesson," arguing that smoothness and continuity of the
lesson contributed to overall engagement with the lesson.

Particular instructional methods may juxtapose instructional settings in such a way that transitions are not smoothly
made. Within-class grouping provides an excellent example of
the difficulty that transitions between instructional activities can
create. In this method, three groups are typically formed in the
class. While the teacher works directly with one group, the
other two groups must work independently on assignments,
usually "Ditto" sheets. Many observations of classroom behavior during this sort of grouping arrangement have found that
student engagement is markedly reduced while students are
working independently on seatwork.

Engagement during seatwork may be less because it is an
inherently uninteresting format. Engagement may also be lower
during seatwork because of the lack of direct supervision and
close monitoring of the teacher.

Another problem with seatwork is that it is often not pertinent to the lesson (Anderson *et al.*, 1985). In particular because
teachers feel the pressure to divide their time evenly among
the three groups, they may give students exercises for which
they are not yet prepared to work independently. Students may
need additional clarification or correction but can get none
because the teacher is instructing one of the other groups. In
the case of within-class grouping, the transition from direct
instruction to independent seatwork may be bumpy (not
smooth) because there was no phase of "guided practice" to
ease the transition.

In general, because of the difficulty of making smooth
transitions between settings, we assume that methods with

fewer transitions will have higher engagement rates. Whole-class instruction, for example, will have higher overall rates of student engagement than within-class grouping methods.

The amount and pace of instruction and student time-on-task are only part of the picture of how learning transpires in classrooms. Without considering the quality of the time spent, we will have only a partial vision of what goes on in classrooms. Quality of instruction in this discussion is primarily gauged by the appropriateness of the lesson for the learner. Was the lesson too easy or too difficult? Did the lesson cover new material or review old but vaguely remembered material? Was the lesson interesting or boring? Quality of instruction, then, is a measure that applies to a learner; it is essentially a measure of the extent to which he or she can learn from the lesson.

Grouping methods and instructional arrangements affect the quality of instruction, but the nature of the effect depends upon the instructional method. In whole-class instruction, because there is one pace and one lesson, the material is often not appropriate for both the advanced and the below-average students. Quality of instruction is thereby diminished for above-average and below-average students in whole-class instruction because of inappropriate pace.

The quality of instruction may also be reduced under individualized instruction although pace and level of instruction are matched to student needs. The problem with quality when individualized instruction is used is that checking for comprehension may be poorly done—that is, the instruction–feedback–corrective loop is often defective. Thus, although individualized instruction solves one problem with quality of instruction, it creates other problems that diminish the overall quality.

Within-class grouping methods may have a better chance of providing quality instruction that either whole-class or individualized methods because there is at least some matching of pace and level and some provision of the necessary loop of instruction, feedback and corrective. The quality depends upon how finely a match of instructional level and presentation is needed and the extent to which seatwork is integrated with instruction.

Grouping strategies affect student effort and contribute to the formation of self-concept of ability (Rosenholtz and Simpson, 1984). The effect of the grouping strategy depends upon the comparisons created and the salience of those comparisons within the classroom. In classrooms with a single task structure and a single reward system (i.e., whole-class instruction), the salience of the instructional group is greater than in multitask and multidimensional classrooms. The nature of instructional tasks within these groups and the nature of the reward system for performance on these tasks forge a status system associated with relative position of a student within the group. In turn, these elements become key determinants of the formation of self-concept of ability.

Student effort depends upon the probability that the student has for success and the incentive value of the reward for success. Grouping strategies affect these two parameters directly and indirectly. The indirect effects work through the effect of pace of instruction relative to student ability and to the capacity to benefit from that pace of instruction. With constant effort, the chance of success diminishes as difficulty increases. Difficulty increases as pace outdistances capacity to keep up with the pace of instruction. The probability of success for a low-ability student is highest when the pace of instruction is matched to his level. Thus, low-ability students in within-class ability settings should have a greater chance for success than their counterparts in whole-class heterogeneous settings, and most likely in tracked classrooms because the teacher can pay better attention to their individual learning requirements.

The incentive value of success depends upon the norms in the classroom affecting its value and the chance of success. Both students who never have a chance to achieve and those who achieve at a constant pace may find little incentive value in the reward system. The number of salient dimensions in the classroom for which there are rewards and recognition (achievement in academics being just one) also affects the incentive value of the reward. Achievement is singularly important as a status dimension in classrooms where single task structures are used and where information about performance is public and readily visible.

Methods of instruction, by altering the composition of the comparison group for rewards, contribute to the formation of student effort. In tracked classes, low-ability students may have an equal chance for success, but the incentive value of the rewards is nonexistent because the peer group devalues its operation. In within-class ability grouping, the probability of success for low-achieving students should be greater than in whole-class methods as instruction is closer to the level from which they benefit. The value of the reward for these students is unclear, however. It depends upon whether the relevant comparison group for these students is the whole class or their particular instructional grouping. There is evidence that the comparison group is the whole class (Rosenholtz and Simpson, 1984), which seems reasonable since students spend the majority of the school day with their classmates, not their reading group. If this is true, then low-ability students in these classrooms, despite their better chance for success within their groups, may still demonstrate lower effort because the rewards for their effort are based on the distribution of achievement for the entire classroom. Individualized models assume that effort will be high because of the accommodation of the method to rate and level, thus making chance for success very high. But the incentive value of success is probably diminished in these systems. Typically, there is no group-based incentive to drive the method, and the inherent interest value of the materials, or incentive through learning, is often diminished by dull, unclear, and inappropriate materials.

Mastery learning attempts to deal with the issue of probability of success by modifying the student's rate of learning and previous knowledge level. However, there is no convincing evidence that in fact mastery learning, as typically implemented, has been able to reduce differences in learning rates (Arlin, 1984).

INSTRUCTIONAL METHOD AND ABILITY LEVEL

The preceding discussion highlights in a general way the effects of instructional method on time, quality, and effort. In this section, we consider in more detail how the various methods affect these components for students of differing ability levels.

The time-use patterns of students of differing ability are affected by instructional methods. The amount of instructional time, the pace, and the engagement rates are all typically lower in low-ability tracked classes than in high-ability tracked classes. The greater incidence of disruptions, off-task related behaviors, and lack of norms supportive of academic achievement contribute to the lower time-use patterns in low-ability tracked classrooms.

In classes in which within-class ability grouping is used, students of differing abilities typically receive the same amounts of instructional time but the pace of instruction is varied. High-ability students are typically on task more during independent seatwork than are low-ability students. Whole-class instruction, by definition, holds students to the same instructional time and pace. Observational studies indicate that lower-ability students are engaged less often in the lesson than are average or high-ability students.

Individualized instruction theoretically would provide all students the same amount of instructional time. However, because low-ability students may have greater difficulty in working independently, or may have greater difficulty because of the inappropriateness of material for their reading level, they may spend a greater portion of their time waiting for assistance and clarification than do high-ability students. Higher-ability students, able to proceed at their own pace, will accordingly have a more rapid pace of instruction. Engagement rates may differ because high-ability students may be better able to work without direct supervision, correctives, and feedback.

Under mastery learning, low-ability students receive more instructional time than students who pass the mastery test.

Students who pass the mastery test typically do enrichment activities while the ones who did not pass receive corrective instruction. Instructional pace during instruction is the same. Consequently, mastery learning, because it gears instructional progress of the entire class to its achievement distribution, will be relatively more appropriate for low-ability, then average, and finally high-ability students.

Under tracking, the curriculum is often differentiated so that high-ability students receive a substantively enriched and complex curriculum while lower-ability students concentrate on basic skills. Teacher motivation and effort are probably high in high-ability classes as well. In fact, teachers may be rewarded by being assigned to teach high-ability classes. With tracking of students into homogeneous groups, student effort in the low-ability classrooms is diminished primarily because the incentive value of success is reduced. Peer norms often do not favor academic success in this environment so that although the chance for success may be greater, student effort is not greater because there are few salient incentives for success.

In whole-class heterogeneous classes wherein a single pace of instruction is used, both the high- and low-ability students may find instruction inappropriate. High-ability students may already have mastered the material while low-ability students may be unable to benefit from the lesson. Whole-class instruction is therefore probably most appropriate to the average student in the classroom. Whole-class heterogeneous grouping, on the other hand, diminishes the chance for success for the low-ability student because there is one reward structure operating in the classroom. The low-ability student's performance is measured by the same yardstick as the high-ability student's, so that the chance for success is diminished. The incentive value of the reward is probably high because the class norms favor achievement.

Because within-class grouping and individualization vary the pace and content of instruction to suit the needs of the ability groups, the appropriateness of instruction should be roughly comparable for all students in these methods. Student effort for low-ability students in classes using within-class ability grouping may be greater both because the incentives for success are greater and the likelihood of being successful is greater.

It has been suggested that student effort depends upon the chance of success and the incentive value of success. The method of grouping students and of delivering instruction affects both these factors.

In Table 1, we summarize this discussion of the major ways in which instructional method affects time use, quality, and student effort by ability level of the student.

NUMERICAL ESTIMATES OF EFFECTS OF METHOD ON TIME, QUALITY, AND EFFORT

Carroll's formulation of learning as a function of time needed and time spent is the basis for the model of learning used here. Time spent is operationalized as the product time $\times$ quality $\times$ effort. Time needed is seen to depend largely upon student aptitude for the task.

In this section, we provide numerical estimates for the time spent and time needed parameters in the model for students of differing abilities under contrasting instructional methods. In attaching estimates to these methods for students of different abilities, we assume that overall the achievement effects of these methods are roughly comparable. This assumption is consistent with the available evidence contrasting the effectiveness of alternative methods of instruction. The estimates for effects of method for students of different abilities follows the discussion just presented. Of course, research to date has not provided empirical estimates on which all these estimates may be based. The estimates used here are simply numerical values attached to our assumptions and available research of how these methods operate.

Table 2 attaches numerical estimates to time spent, quality, effort, and time needed parameters for students of different

Table 1
Effects of Instructional Method on Time Needed and Time Spent by
Ability of Student

Methods	Time		Instructional quality		Student effort	
		Amount Pace Engagement		Appropriateness Curriculum Teacher Motivation		Success Incentive
Tracking (T)	H:L	more time and engagement, faster pace	H:L	curriculum more difficult; teacher motivation, quality better	H:L	greater effort; class norms support achievement
Within-class grouping (G)	H:L	same time, more engagement, faster pace	H:L	curriculum, quality, teacher motivation same	H:L	greater effort; group norms support achievement
	L(G):	L(T) more engagement, faster pace	L(G):	L(T) curriculum, quality, teacher motivation better	L(G):	L(T): greater effort, same chance of success
Whole class (W)	H.L	same time, same pace, more engagement	L(W):	L(G) curriculum more difficult	L(W):	L(G) differential in not determinable, No Effect on same chance of success
Individual (I)	H:L	more time, faster pace	H:L	same content, quality, teacher motivation	H:L	same effort, same reward, same chance of success
Mastery Learning (M)	H:L	less time, same pace	H:L	same content, quality, teacher motivation	H:L	same effort, same reward, same chance of success

Table 2
Hypothetical Degree of Learning Using Alternate Instructional Methods for High-ability, Average, Low-ability Students

Method, student ability	Percentage of time of instruction	Days of instruction per year	Percentage of appropriate time	Percentage of student effort	Time spent (days)	Time needed (days)	Degree of learning	+/− days
Whole class
High	.90	162	.70	.75	85	50	1.00	+35
Average	.90	162	.80	.80	103	75	1.00	+53
Low	.90	162	.70	.75	85	100	.85	−15
Tracked class
High	.90	162	.80	.80	103	50	1.00	+53
Average	.90	162	.80	.80	103	75	1.00	+28
Low	.70	126	.70	.70	62	100	.62	−38
Within-class
High	.80	144	.85	.75	92	50	1.00	+42
Average	.80	144	.85	.75	92	75	1.00	+17
Low	.80	144	.85	.70	86	100	.86	−14
Individualized
High	.70	126	.80	.80	80	50	1.00	+30
Average	.70	126	.80	.80	80	75	1.00	+5
Low	.70	126	.80	.80	80	100	.80	−20
Mastery Learning
High	.75	135	.70	.80	76	50	1.00	+26
Average	.75	135	.80	.80	86	75	1.00	+11
Low	.80	144	.85	.80	97	100	.97	−3

aptitudes under different methods. We start by assuming that all students have 180 days available for instruction in the school year. To advance through one academic year's worth of instruction, we assume that students must spend varying amounts of time. Low-ability students need more time than do average-ability students who need more time than high-ability students. We assume here that the ratio of time needed is 2:1 for low-ability to high-ability students. The difference may in fact be greater. Next, we assume that in order to master a year's worth of academic material the lower-ability students must spend 100 days. Although this figure may seem low in comparison to the 180 days available, the figure of 100 days of instructional time is fairly consistent with the amount of time schools actually use for instruction. If the low-ability students need 100 days, then the high-ability students who need half this time will accordingly need 50 days to master the curriculum.

In Table 2, the second and third columns provide estimates of the number of instructional "days" after reducing available time by the management time and other noninstructional time associated with a method. Using whole-class methods, for example, the time spent on instruction is set at about 90 percent because little management time is required. Within-class grouping has a lower rate because management time is needed to group and regroup students and for teacher transitions between activities. Column 3 of Table 2 thus provides estimates of the number of instructional "days" under these methods.

The quality of instruction is set as a proportion of the time during which instruction is appropriate for the learner. Whole-class instruction is seen to be most appropriate for the average student and equally as inappropriate for the high- and low-ability students. The quality of instruction for within-class grouping is comparable for all students as is quality for individualized instruction. Mastery learning is argued to have higher quality for low-ability students the only method for which this assumption is made.

Student effort here may be thought of as the proportion of time during which the student pays attention to the lesson.

Student effort and attention are reduced most in within-class ability grouping because of the lower attention during independent seatwork.

Time spent is the product of quality, quantity, and effort. This is measured by days available, proportion of days in instruction, proportion of appropriate instruction, and proportion of time students pay attention to instruction—our operationalization of effort × quality × time. Here time spent ranges from a high of 103 to a low of 62 days.

The degree of learning is the ratio of time spent to time needed. For students who spend more time than they need, the ratio is set at 1.0 because it is assumed that under this condition the students are in fact not going to learn additional materials, but simply what is presented to them. The last column (+/−) indicates the discrepancy (over or under) between days spent and days needed. All models appear to be deficient for low-ability students, with tracking the most deficient. The results reflected in Table 2 conform in a general way to the pattern of empirical results reported in studies contrasting these alternative methods. For example, the different methods appear to produce about comparable results for different levels of ability with the exception of tracking, in which low-ability students are relatively disadvantaged.

Table 2 illustrates how different degrees of time, quality, and student effort, housed in distinct methods, may in fact yield similar achievement distributions. Quite different processes may then produce comparable achievement results given present methods of organizing students for instruction.

What are the potentials and difficulties for improving the efficiency of time, quality, and effort under the different methods? How are the three components related? Will more time, for example, decrease student effort? Are these results likely to be the same for all students? What changes in the methods would obtain minimum competency and would raise the standards for all students?

It is important for issues of equity to understand how the different instructional strategies work and their potential for obtaining the educational goals we establish. Put another way, it is important to understand the limitations and possibilities of our methods for instruction in pursuit of larger societal goals. Do we have instructional strategies that can deliver the goals of equity and excellence?

If it were possible to remedy the various deficits of the particular methods, and to make instruction efficient, what would the outcomes be for students of high ability, of average ability, of low ability? Would a particular technique serve to raise the average achievement score and reduce the variance? Or would it raise the average score and increase the variance? What sort of goals do we have for distributional properties of achievement measures? What does minimum competency as a goal have to say for choices between different sets of outcomes? Is a treatment that raises achievement for all and also raises the variance preferable? It is possible, although optimistic, that at some foreseeable date there may be sufficient information about the workings of different classroom processes that such questions can be more than mere hypothetical queries, as they are here. In the next paragraphs, we address two issues related to equity and outcomes of schooling: the operation of different instructional methods in pursuit of the attainment of minimum competencies and the raising of academic standards.

THE USE OF EXISTING METHODS FOR ATTAINMENT OF MINIMUM STANDARDS

In the next paragraphs, we ask how each of these methods might be altered so that minimum achievement standards may be approached. In these exercises, a standard of minimum competency is achieved when the time needed and time spent for the low achievers is comparable. We use the figure of 100 days of time spent and time needed for low-ability students as the definition of meeting minimum standards. In Tables 3 to 7 the effects of altering various instructional components are examined for the different methods. The general strategy used here is to increase the use of time or quality of materials or student effort until the desired 100 days of time spent is reached.

In Table 3, we carry out changes in pace and time for whole-class instruction. By lowering the pace of instruction to benefit the low-achieving students in the class (second group of estimates), we also increase the quality of instruction, effort, and attention for this group (see strategy 2). Increasing the school year by 20 days, without altering quality and effort (third set of estimates) does increase the degree of learning for these students but does not result in the desired level of change. The hypothetical effects of changing instructional pace and school time length are shown in the last set of estimates.

Table 4 carries out a similar exercise for high-, average-, and low-ability students in tracked classes. Given the efficiencies we have chosen for this method, which seem consistent with the empirical findings of the effects of tracking on low-ability students, reaching the goal of 100 days of time spent, our minimum competency goal, is rather difficult. Only after changing the number of days in the school year, the amount of the school year to be used for instruction, teacher motivation, pace of instruction, and student effort is there a sufficient boost in time spent to increase the days over the necessary 100 days needed by these students. If tracking is to be used, then, changes in the incentive structure as well as the amount of instructional time will have to be made to achieve minimum competency goals. The low incentive value of success in tracked classes is a major difficulty. Segregation of students contributes to this lack of incentive value. If segregation of students remains a part of the structure, then other ways of increasing the incentive for success will have to be introduced for this method to be workable. Possibilities include team rewards and token economies.

Within-class ability grouping looks more promising as a technique for increasing achievement for low-ability students. The percent of the time that can be used for instruction can be increased by better use of methods to increase teaching time (e.g., easing transitions into groups by posting work ahead of time for students to do as they come into the group). The quality

Table 3

Altering Whole-class Instruction to Achieve Minimum Standards

Method, student ability	Percentage of time of instruction	Days of instruction per year	Percentage of appropriate time	Percentage of student effort	Time spent (days)	Time needed (days)	Degree of learning	+/− days
Whole class (original)								
High	.90	162	.70	.75	85	50	1.00	+35
Average	.90	162	.80	.80	103	75	1.00	+53
Low	.90	162	.70	.75	85	100	.85	−15
Changing pace of instruction to benefit slowest group								
High	.90	162	.70	.75	85	50	1.00	+35
Average	.90	162	.70	.75	85	75	1.00	+10
Low	.90	162	.80	.80	104	100	1.00	+ 4
Changing length of school year from 180 to 200 days								
High	.90	180	.70	.75	95	50	1.00	+35
Average	.90	180	.80	.80	115	75	1.00	+10
Low	.90	180	.70	.75	95	100	.95	− 5
Changing pace and length								
High	.90	180	.70	.75	95	50	1.00	+35
Average	.90	180	.70	.80	101	75	1.00	+26
Low	.90	180	.80	.75	108	100	1.00	8

Table 4

Altering Tracked Class Assignment to Achieve Minimum Standards

Method, student ability	Percentage of time of instruction	Days of instruction per year	Percentage of appropriate time	Percentage of student effort	Time spent (days)	Time needed (days)	Degree of learning	+/- days
Tracked (original)								
High	.90	162	.80	.80	103	50	1.00	+53
Average	.90	162	.80	.80	103	75	1.00	+28
Low	.70	126	.70	.70	62	100	.62	-38
Change percentage of time used for instruction								
High	.90	162	.80	.80	103	50	1.00	+53
Average	.90	162	.80	.80	103	75	1.00	+28
Low	.80	144	.70	.70	70	100	.70	-30
Change percentage of time used and teacher motivation								
High	.90	162	.80	.80	103	50	1.00	+53
Average	.90	162	.80	.80	103	75	1.00	+28
Low	.80	144	.75	.70	76	100	.76	-24

Change instructional time, teacher motivation, and incentive system

High	.90	162	.80	103	50	1.00	+53
Average	.90	162	.80	103	75	1.00	+28
Low	.80	144	.75	81	100	.81	−19

Change time, teacher motivation, incentive system, and content covered

High	.90	162	.80	103	50	1.00	+53
Average	.90	162	.80	103	75	1.00	+28
Low	.80	144	.80	86	100	.86	−14

Change time, teacher motivation, incentive system, and content covered, 200 days

High	.90	180	.80	115	50	1.00	+65
Average	.90	180	.80	115	75	1.00	+40
Low	.80	180	.75	108	100	1.00	+ 8

Change only length of school term 180 to 200 days

High	.90	180	.80	115	50	1.00	+65
Average	.90	180	.80	115	75	1.00	+40
Low	.70	140	.70	68	100	.68	−32

of instruction, too, can possibly be increased in these classes by tailoring seatwork more carefully to a student's skill level. In the fourth set of figures in Table 5, which shows the effect of increasing the amount of time used for instruction, the quality of instruction, and student effort, the 100 days of time spent is realized for these students.

Alterations to individualized instruction are presented in Table 6. The major problem with individualized instruction is the need for management time to deliver the method. However, increasing the percent of time used for instruction is not sufficient to reach minimum competency goals, given the other assumptions about the quality of instruction and student effort. Increasing the quality of the materials, which may also help to increase student interest and effort, shows that the time spent and time needed for low-ability students can reach minimum competency levels.

Finally, changes in the delivery of mastery learning are considered in Table 7. The literature on mastery learning indicates that this technique is effective but that it requires additional time. This is reflected in the numerical exercises by increasing the percentage of time used for instruction from .80 to .85. The quality of instruction and student effort were not changed in this example.

Minimum competency testing is a workable means of evaluating and improving instructional effectiveness for this segment of the school population, but as an agenda for general school reform and rejuvenation this strategy is too limited and too narrow in focus and intention. Therefore, the focus on attainment of basic skills serves to reduce, not enlarge, the vision of what is possible. Thus, both for symbolic reasons and because these tests define the curriculum as taught, minimum competency attainment is a limited goal for school improvement. If we enlarge our view of school improvement to include raising standards for all students, the next issue is the extent to which this goal can be accomplished by existing major instructional methods.

Table 5
Altering Within-class Grouping to Attain Minimum Standards

Method. student ability	Percentage of time of instruction	Days of instruction per year	Percentage of appropriate time	Percentage of student effort	Time spent (days)	Time needed (days)	Degree of learning	+/− days
Within-class (original)								
High	.80	144	.85	.75	92	50	1.00	+42
Average	.80	144	.85	.75	92	75	1.00	+17
Low	.80	144	.85	.70	86	100	.86	−14
Change percentage of instructional time								
High	.85	153	.85	.75	97	50	1.00	+47
Average	.85	153	.85	.75	97	75	1.00	+22
Low	.85	153	.85	.70	91	100	.86	− 9
Change percentage of instructional time and increase quality								
High	.85	153	.90	.75	103	50	1.00	+53
Average	.85	153	.90	.75	103	75	1.00	+28
Low	.85	153	.90	.70	96	100	.96	− 4
Change percentage of instructional time and increase quality and effort								
High	.85	153	.90	.75	103	50	1.00	+53
Average	.85	153	.90	.75	103	75	1.00	+28
Low	.85	153	.90	.75	96	103	1.00	+ 3

Table 6
Altering Individualized Instruction to Attain Minimum Standards

Method, student ability	Percentage of time of instruction	Days of instruction per year	Percentage of appropriate time	Percentage of student effort	Time spent (days)	Time needed (days)	Degree of learning	+/− days
Individual (original)								
High	.70	126	.80	.80	80	50	1.00	+30
Average	.70	126	.80	.80	80	75	1.00	+5
Low	.70	126	.80	.80	80	100	.80	−20
Change amount of instructional time								
High	.80	144	.80	.80	92	50	1.00	+42
Average	.80	144	.80	.80	92	75	1.00	+17
Low	.80	144	.80	.80	92	100	.92	−8
Change amount of instructional time and increase quality								
High	.80	144	.90	.80	103	50	1.00	+53
Average	.80	144	.90	.80	103	75	1.00	+28
Low	.80	144	.90	.80	103	100	.92	3

Table 7
Altering Mastery Learning to Attain Minimum Standards

Method, student ability	Percentage of time of instruction	Days of instruction per year	Percentage of appropriate time	Percentage of student effort	Time spent (days)	Time needed (days)	Degree of learning	+/− days
Mastery (original)								
High	.75	135	.70	.80	76	50	1.00	+26
Average	.75	135	.80	.80	86	75	1.00	+11
Low	.80	144	.85	.80	.97	100	97	− 3
Change percentage of time used								
High	.80	144	.70	.80	80	50	1.00	+30
Average	.80	144	.80	.80	92	75	1.00	+18
Low	.85	153	.85	.80	104	100	.97	+ 4

THE USE OF EXISTING METHODS TO RAISE STANDARDS

Regardless of disagreements over whether the schools of today are better, worse, or about the same as schools some thirty years ago, there is generally an agreement that higher standards and more difficult core courses should be incorporated into the common curriculum for all students. The difficult issue is how this can be accomplished. Can we have minimum competency and a core curriculum and raise standards all at the same time? What accommodation to classroom practices will have to be made in order to do this?

To examine this question, we start by formulating what increasing standards would mean for time spent and time needed in school. Increasing standards means that more effort and time will have to be put into school work, so in our model we have used time needed as the parameter reflecting increases in standards. In Table 8, we have changed time needed for all students to 100 days. For a high-ability student to need the same instructional time as a low-ability student, the material must be either more difficult or there must be more of it. Table 8 is interesting because it indicates the deficiencies of the various methods for providing enough time given these new definitions of time needed.

Does the combination of parameters that accomplish minimum competency allow for higher standards? When one looks at Tables 3 through 7 at the change that first produced this standard for the low-ability students, the difficulties in attaining these twin goals become apparent. In whole-class instruction with heterogeneous groups, lowering the pace achieved the minimum competency, but it will not raise standards for the middle and high-ability students. In tracking, the original system already allowed the high and middle students to attain these standards; the difficulty is in getting the low-tracked classes to attain minimum competency, which required changes in all the parameters plus lengthening of the school term. Within-class grouping and individualization could accomplish these

Table 8

Hypothetical Degree of Learning Using Alternate Instructional Methods for High-ability, Average, and Low-ability Students When Standards Have Been Raised

Method, student ability	Percentage of time of instruction	Days of instruction per year	Percentage of appropriate time	Percentage of student effort	Time spent (days)	Time needed (days)	Degree of learning	+/− days
Whole class								
High	.90	162	.70	.75	85	100	.85	− 15
Average	.90	162	.80	.80	103	100	1.00	+ 53
Low	.90	162	.70	.75	85	100	.85	− 15
Tracked								
High	.90	162	.80	.80	103	100	1.00	+ 3
Average	.90	162	.80	.80	103	100	1.00	+ 3
Low	.70	126	.70	.70	62	100	.62	− 38
Within-class								
High	.80	144	.85	.75	92	100	.92	− 8
Average	.80	144	.85	.75	92	100	.92	− 8
Low	.80	144	.85	.70	86	100	.86	− 14
Individual								
High	.70	126	.80	.80	80	100	.80	− 20
Average	.70	126	.80	.80	80	100	.80	− 20
Low	70	126	.80	.80	80	100	.80	− 20
Mastery								
High	.75	135	.70	.80	76	100	.76	− 24
Average	.75	135	.80	.80	86	100	.86	− 14
Low	.80	144	.85	.80	97	100	.97	− 3

goals of minimum competency and raising standards with improvements in student effort. However, it is not clear how student effort can be improved in within-class grouping strategies. The strength of the method is that it allows for differentiated curricula, but this strength creates status differentiation along ability lines which may reduce the gains in effectiveness for appropriateness of instruction. One strategy to help solve this problem might be to have rewards to heterogenously composed groups, where the contribution of low-ability students would be integral and equivalent to their higher-achieving classmates. Some strategy for group-based rewards in the context of within-class ability grouping may help to sustain effort for low-achieving students. But status differences are likely to remain apparent and consequential to students. It is a matter of degree, not of existence.

Moreover, within-class ability grouping requires considerably more teacher energy and preparation than the other methods. To follow this method properly, teachers are actively teaching most of the time. For example, in our comparison of time use under ability-grouped and whole-class methods, we found that ability-grouping teachers were actually teaching some 90 percent of their time, in comparison to 77 percent of the time for whole-class methods (Slavin and Karweit, 1984).

Another approach to providing enough time to meet changing standards and minimum competency goals would be to vary the amount of instructional time allocated to different groups. Low-ability students would be given the additional time required for corrective instruction. Targetting instructional resources in this fashion would certainly be less expensive and potentially more effective than increasing resources such as school time statewide or nationwide. Its effectiveness would depend upon how closely the programs are coordinated with the regular curriculum and how much additional time is actually needed for remediation. New efficiencies may be realized in remediation by providing carefully targetted instruction, strong incentive systems for achievement, and interesting or novel delivery systems (e.g., computers). However, the major difficulty is the need to coordinate remediation efforts with regular classroom instruction. The failure of this coordination is clearly seen in the case of pull-out programs which supplant rather than supplement instruction to the questionable benefit of the students. Unless detailed, day-to-day coordination is seriously pursued, remediation and corrective instruction efforts are likely to end up as additional evidence for the futility of compensatory education.

Another strategy with school time would be selectively to increase the amount of time in school commensurate with time needed. Schools could have a baseline number of days in operation, say 180, for which all students were required to be in attendance. Additional time could then be added to this for remediation. For example, there could be intensive summer schooling lasting for 40 days. Students would attend either the entire 40 days or until they had passed specific mastery requirements.

Increasing school time in this fashion may not be as beneficial as increasing school time on a daily basis to allow for remediation and enrichment. Certainly, there are benefits to remediation on the day the misunderstanding arose, not six months later. Summer school may then be more of a last-ditch sort of effort to catch students up before retaining them in a grade.

There may be objections to adding more time for slower-achieving students as an inequitable practice for their more advantaged classmates. But if resources are increased for all students, then we are back in the same situation of discrepancies in outcomes for the same inputs.

Short of allocating more time, reducing some of the subjects taught, or dramatically increasing the efficiency of instruction through new technologies, the twin goals of raising standards and assuring minimum competencies are more in competition with one another at present than in coexistence. Instruction as presently practiced does not happily accommodate these two goals simultaneously. Moreover, applying

estimates for reasonable improvements to the instructional efficiencies of these different strategies does not suggest that these
two goals can easily be accomplished.

If this analysis is correct, it suggests that group instruction
and student diversity will present a continuing dilemma for
school organization, only part of which is resolved by addressing efficiency issues. Students differ. Paying attention to differences is necessary for instructional effectiveness. Paying
attention to differences also helps create and maintain a status
system based upon these differences. Grouping strategies are
one way to organize students around differences by attempting
to minimize them. In the process, status differences among
students are increased. Although this exaggeration of student
status differences is not a valued outcome of schooling, it is
seen as a necessary consequence of instruction in groups. These
side effects of grouping occur because of the nature of rewards
and incentives in the instructional group, not because of the
efficiency of the grouping strategy. Therefore, increasing efficiency within the same basic models will not address these
concerns.

It is interesting that one of the sharpest foci in classroom
reform has been on classroom time use, which is primarily an
efficiency and management issue. But there are limits on how
much these factors can be increased without expecting other
negative side effects. For example, student attention rates are
anywhere in the range of 75 to 85 percent. Some of the off-task
behavior may be needed as a break from instructional time.

Student motivation and effort have been viewed as internal, unchangeable attributes not affected by the externalities of
the classroom. This outlook on classrooms and students provides a very limited menu for improvement. Effective instruction is the product of simultaneous attention to time, quality,
and student effort. Of these, student effort and attention are
probably least understood. Classroom practices also are probably least varied along this dimension. Certainly future elab-
orations of the basic instructional models that have been

described here must consider alternative and workable ways to evaluate and reward students.

SUMMARY AND CONCLUSION

This chapter has examined the links between methods of organizing students for instruction and issues of standards and diversity. It began by noting that classrooms are singularly important locations for understanding the operation and consequences of our assumptions about equity, student diversity, and standards. We have examined how five major methods of grouping students for instruction affect important mediating variables that define students' learning—time, quality of instruction, and effort. Different grouping strategies were shown to define how and to what extent student differences are acknowledged in the daily workings of the classroom. The grouping strategies affect the use of time, the appropriateness of instruction, and student attention and effort. We have argued that existing grouping strategies are inadequate for achieving the twin educational goals of raising standards and achieving minimum competencies.

Fundamental rearrangements of classrooms and schools may be necessary to accomplish these goals. In particular, a variable time structure in which students progress not by fixed grade levels but by achievement standards may be a more realistic approach to providing appropriate instruction. Such an approach might mix together students of quite different ages but of comparable learning levels for some part of their instructional day. This notion of heterogeneous grouping by age to create relatively homogeneous instructional groups is certainly not a new idea, but one that should be reconsidered (e.g., Joplin plan). Certainly, as the movement toward exit and entry exams for promotion indicates, the notion of promotion on the basis of specific mastery is not entirely unacceptable. Carried to its logical extension, schools would be organized not by grade level but competency or mastery level. This approach is a simple idea, but its implementation would radically transform schools as we know them today.

REFERENCES

Anderson, Linda, Nancy Brubaker, Janet Alleman-Brooks, and Gerald Duffy. 1985. "A qualitative study of seatwork in first-grade classrooms." *Elementary School Journal* 86:123–140.

Arlin, Marshall. 1984. "Time variability in mastery learning." *American Educational Research Journal* 21:103–120.

Barr, Rebecca and Robert Dreeben. 1983. *How Schools Work*. Chicago: University of Chicago Press.

Carroll, John. 1963. "A model of school learning." *Teachers College Record* 64(8):723–733.

Dahloff, Urban. 1971. *Ability Grouping, Content Validity, and Curriculum Process Analysis*. New York: Teachers College Press, Columbia University.

Kounin, Jacab. 1970. *Discipline and Group Management in Classrooms*. New York: Holt, Rinehart and Winston.

Rosenholtz, Susan and Carl Simpson. 1984. "The formation of ability conceptions: developmental trend or social construction?" *Review of Educational Research* 54:31–63.

Slavin, Robert and Nancy Karweit. 1984. "Effects of whole-class, ability grouped and individualized instruction on mathematics achievement." *American Educational Research Journal* 22:351–367.

CHAPTER 5

The Organizational Differentiation of Students in Schools as an Opportunity Structure

AAGE B. SØRENSEN

INTRODUCTION

A large part of the sociological research on educational processes in the last twenty years has been concerned with "educational opportunities." Increasing and equalizing opportunities have been goals used to justify much educational policy making and educational research. The title of the research report that marked the beginning of modern large-scale quantitative sociological research on education—*Equality of Educational Opportunity* (Coleman *et al.*, 1966)—contains the three most frequently found

Aage B. Sørensen • Department of Sociology, Harvard University, Cambridge, MA 02138. The research reported here was supported in part by the Royalty Fund of the Center for Educational Research, University of Wisconsin-Madison.

words in research proposals and research reports by sociologists in the two decades since then.

Many words important for the legitimization of individual or social action like *love*, *equality*, and *justice* are perhaps most useful when their meaning is left vague. Noboby in America, whether liberal or conservative, will be against equality of opportunity in principle. When the term is left sufficiently vague, being for equality of opportunity means being for almost any policy that improves the lot of somebody. In the research arena, equality of opportunity has been defined quite vaguely to allow a great diversity of research activities to be seen as addressing this topic in one form or another; it has been quite accurately believed, at least until the Reagan years, that few will be against funding research for something that everybody wants.

Opportunity is a key sociological concept also outside of the sociology of education. The concept presumably refers to some property associated with social structures that should be identifiable and measurable. But the concept of opportunity is not well defined outside of the educational research arena either. In contrast to other key concepts, such as class, the problem is not one of many competing definitions and conceptualizations. Rather, sociologists usually do not try to define opportunity and equality of opportunity precisely. These terms seem to be taken as primitives, in no need of further definition. In non-educational uses as well there appears to be some usefulness in keeping the meaning of these terms vague.

Recognizing the usefulness of vagueness about key terms does not mean that it is never useful to be precise. In fact, this chapter will argue that important insights can be gained from being precise about the terms *opportunity* and *equality of opportunity*. The basic ideas are not specific to education, but it is instructive to develop them in this particular context. Doing so will also cast some light on some long-standing controversies in the sociology of education about the impact of organizational differentiation or tracking on learning and on the existence of school effects in general.

The chapter will develop a concept of opportunities for learning as being a key determinant of how much learning takes place in schools. These opportunities for learning in turn are systematically structured by the curriculum differentiation associated with tracking and other forms of organizational differentiation of students in schools. The relation between organizational factors and opportunities for learning creates a contingent relation between student background characteristics and actual academic achievement, the contingencies being created by contextual and organizational factors causing variation among schools in the organizational differentiation of students.

The ideas developed here imply that there can be much systematic variation between schools in amount of learning that cannot be accounted for by variation in student-body characteristics. This has not been recognized in earlier quantitative research on school processes primarily because of the lack of adequate specification of the processes that create opportunities for learning in schools. In fact, it can easily be shown that the mechanisms that create opportunities cannot be identified using the conventional cross-sectional models employed in most research on educational attainment and opportunity.

To be precise about the key concepts, I shall first present a specification of how opportunities interact with student characteristics in producing learning. This provides a more precise idea than usual of what is meant by opportunities for learning. Then follows the presentation of the main ideas about the organization of opportunities for learning by characteristics of schools and students.

In addition to these theoretical developments, I shall also present the results of analyses of the first follow-up survey and the base-line survey of the 1980 sophomores in the *High School and Beyond Study*. Although still preliminary, these empirical results support the main ideas, both about the concept of opportunities for learning and about the structure of opportunities.

OPPORTUNITIES FOR LEARNING AND
ACADEMIC ACHIEVEMENT

The concern in this chapter, as in much sociological research
on education, is with analyzing social processes relevant for
academic achievement. Academic achievement is usually measured by some test of what the student has learned up until the
time of testing. Thus, the focus is on outcomes of learning
processes, and much sociological research concerns how families, schools, and classrooms influence these outcomes. We all
know from this research that ability is relevant for how much
a student will learn. In fact, many sociologists have come to
believe that ability is the only thing relevant, if ability is taken
in a broad sense to mean student background characteristics
determined outside of the schools. Ever since *Equality of Educational Opportunity* (Coleman *et al.*, 1966), it has been the conclusion of most research on these matters that what goes on in
schools makes little difference for what students learn.

Formally, at least, it cannot be true that student background characteristics are the only thing relevant for what a
student learns. Students can learn only what they have been
made aware of as a result of teaching, either formally by teachers and books or informally by experiment and experience. If
there is variation in what students are taught, there should be
variation in what they learn—unless students learn nothing of
what is taught. If students learn something, it should be measurable by achievement tests, unless achievement tests are
culture-free ability tests. Presumably tests are not completely
unrelated to what is taught in schools. The conclusion of much
research—that most variation in achievement is explained by
student background—might then mean that there is little variation among schools, classes, and teachers in what is taught.
It may also mean that this research went about measuring things
the wrong way.

In Sørensen and Hallinan (1978) we make the argument
that school and other instructional effects on learning were
measured the wrong way in much sociological research. The

argument was based on a specification of the academic achievement process that, if correct, implies that conventional cross-sectional models are likely to provide misleading information about variation among schools, teachers, and classrooms in what is taught. The key concept in the development of this argument is the concept of opportunities for learning. It is useful to repeat, in a slight reformulation, the development of this concept here.

The basic idea is that students cannot learn what they have not been exposed to in instructional materials and by teachers. The total amount of material presented in some subject, like algebra, we assume to be a quantity, v^*, that will vary among schools, teachers, and classrooms. It will be a function of curricula and of teacher ability and effort. This quantity is then a measure of what a student might learn: it is a measure of his opportunities for learning. It is conceivable that one could obtain direct measures of this quantity from studies of the curricula of individual teachers and observations of their actual instruction. Nobody seems to have attempted this. For purposes of research relying on measures of students' actual achievement, an indirect measure should be obtained. Such a measure can be obtained by specifying mathematically how opportunities for learning and student characteristics interact in producing measurable achievement.

Assume that instruction in a given subject starts at some time, $t' = 0$. By time t a student will have learned some fraction of the material, or utilized some fraction of the opportunities for learning. The amount learned by time t shall be denoted $y(t)$. This quantity, assumed measured with an achievement test, is presumably some function of the characteristics of a student and his opportunities for learning. The characteristics of the individual student that are relevant for the learning of the material we assume measured by a variable, s. The quantity s then is determined by the student's ability and effort. That s is relevant to the amount of material learned, out of what the student has been exposed to, can most simply be expressed as:

$$dy(t) = s \, dv(t) \tag{1}$$

That is, what is learned in some small interval of time is some fraction of what has been taught in that small interval of time, where the fraction learned is determined by s. Equation (1) relates learning to the amount taught in a small interval of time, but we do not have a direct measure of $v(t)$. Nevertheless, empirical analysis can still be done, assuming a particular relation between $v(t)$ and time and then deriving a model in observable quantities for the achievement process.

We propose a very simple relation between $v(t)$ and time t, but one that is nevertheless not unrealistic. We assume that most teaching is the presentation of instructional material, mixing new material with repetition of old material. At the beginning of a curriculum unit, most of the material will be new. At the end, most of the material presented will be repetition of materials already taught. The total amount to be presented is v^*. The amount already presented by time t, that is, $v(t)$, will be assumed to change over time in relation to how much material has already been presented so that the increase in $v(t)$, or $dv(t)$, reaches zero as $v(t)$ approaches v^*. Let $z(t) = dv(t)$; then a convenient formulation of how $z(t)$ changes over time will be:

$$\frac{dz(t)}{dt} = -b'z(t) \tag{2}$$

Integrating this simple differential equation shows that the amount of new material presented in a small period of time, that is, $z(t)$, will be a simple exponential function of time: $z(t) = ke^{-b't}$. The constant k gives the amount of new material presented in the first lesson of the curriculum unit. Without loss of generality, we may set $k = 1$. Integrating $z(t)$ over time provides an expression for $v(t)$, the total amount of material presented by time t. We obtain:

$$v(t) = \frac{1}{b'}[1 - e^{-b't}] \tag{3}$$

At the end of the period of instruction in the material $z(t) = 0$, everything is repetition, and $v(t)$ will equal v^*. It follows that $b' = \dfrac{1}{v^*}$ that b' will reflect the opportunities for learning to which the student has been exposed.

The quantities entering in equation (1) have now been specified and we can derive an expression for how $y(t)$, observable academic achievement in a given subject, depends on the opportunities for learning and the student's ability and effort. Things become a bit simpler if we define $b = -b'$. With this change in notation, inserting (3) in (1) and solving gives:

$$y(t) = \frac{s}{b}[e^{bt} - 1] \qquad (4)$$

This expression assumes that $y(0) = 0$; students learn nothing of what they have not been exposed to. We rarely have observations coinciding with the start of an instructional process. Fortunately, differentiating (4) produces a simple linear differential equation, $\dfrac{dy(t)}{dt} = s + by(t)$. Integrating this equation over an arbitrary period t' to t'' produces:

$$y(t'') = y(t')e^{b(t''-t')} + \frac{s}{b}[e^{b(t''-t')} - 1] \qquad (5)$$

This solution to the differential equation assumes that s remains constant over the period t' to t'', or that ability and effort can be considered unaffected by the learning process in the period considered. This would not be a reasonable assumption for long periods, but it is a useful and not too unrealistic assumption for shorter periods of observation. If one had a single measure of s, equation (5) could be estimated. We do not have such a measure, but a set of indicators of student ability and effort. Assuming these measures to be linearly related to s, that is, $s = \Sigma a_i x_i$, gives:

$$y(t'') = a_0^* + b^* \, y(t') + a_1^* x_1 + a_2^* x_2 + \cdots + a_n^* x_n \qquad (6)$$

Here

$$a_i^* = \frac{a_i}{b} [e^{b(t'' - t')} - 1]$$

and

$$b^* = e^{b(t'' - t')}$$

Equation (6) is a simple lagged model. The derivation of this model here shows that the coefficients to independent variable are a function of the contribution of the variable in question to a student's ability and effort, the length of the interval t' to t'', and of b, the opportunities for learning. The quantity b^*, that is, the coefficient to the lagged achievement measure, is a function of b and the length of the time interval. For identical time intervals, a larger b^* means more opportunities for learning.

Despite the somewhat complicated expressions for the a_i^* coefficients, it is quite simple to solve for the fundamental parameters, a_i and b, as shown by Coleman (1968).

It is useful to show the behavior of (6) as t'' goes to infinity. From (5) with the expansion of s, one obtains:

$$y(\infty) = \sum d_i x_i \qquad (7)$$

where $d_i = \dfrac{-a_i}{b}$. Equation (7) is, of course, the conventional cross-sectional model used in most sociological research on educational processes. It cannot identify the variation in opportunities for learning among schools and instructional groups but confounds such variation with variation in the contribution of independent variables to students' ability and effort.

This section has developed a concept of opportunities for learning from a simple theory of how academic achievement comes about. It remains to be shown that this simple theory is empirically sufficiently adequate to allow for meaningful analysis of opportunities for learning. Clearly, if the concept cannot be identified empirically, it is not useful to construct an elaborate theory of the organization of such opportunities. Some empirical support is presented in Sørensen and Hallinan (1978, 1986). Using the "High School and Beyond" data, support for the ideas is also available.

Measuring Opportunities for Learning

The 1982 follow-up study to the *High School and Beyond* study provides a series of measures of academic achievement for the 1982 seniors who were tested as sophomores in 1980. Using the standardized reading achievement score as the measure of $y(t)$, Table 1 presents results of an OLS estimation of Equation (6) using a composite measure of socioeconomic status (BYSES) and race as independent variables. The model is estimated for those students who in 1980 were reported to be

Table 1

Regression of Reading Achievement in Senior Year on Reading
Achievement in Sophomore Year, Race, and Socioeconomic
Background for Students in Academic and Nonacademic Track

Independent variables	Academic		Nonacademic	
	B	s.e.	B	s.e.
BBREADSD	.647	.033	.526	.023
BYSES	2.063	.433	1.349	.310
RACED	2.544	.785	2.812	.470
Constant	18.815		22.385	
R^2	.470		.370	
N	652		1336	

Test for same slopes in both groups $F = 14.118$ $p < .001$

Note: Dependent variable is FYREADSD, reading achievement in senior year. BBREADSD is reading achievement in sophomore year. BYSES is composite measure of socioeconomic background. RACED is dummy variable for race (white = 1, nonwhite = 0).

in the academic track and for those who were reported to be in some other track. A 15 percent random sample of the full sample of public school students is used in this analysis. Private school students are excluded so that differences between academic and nonacademic track are not thought to be differences due to a public versus private distinction (in private schools disproportionally many students are in academic track).

One should, of course, expect there to be more opportunities for learning in academic tracks than in nonacademic tracks reflecting differences in curricula and perhaps also in teacher characteristics. It is easily shown that there are indeed differences in academic achievement between the two tracks. But part of this difference presumably reflects differences between the students in the two tracks. We need to separate the achievement difference due to differences in student characteristics from those due to different opportunities for learning. As shown above, the differences in opportunities are measured by the coefficient to the lagged measure of achievement. Indeed, b^* for academic track is .647 as opposed to .526 for nonacademic track, or $b(=\log b^*)$ is $-.435$ in academic track and $-.642$ in nonacademic track so that growth in achievement is more constrained in the nonacademic track, reflecting the fewer opportunities for learning.

An important implication of the conception presented here of the mechanism that translates opportunities for learning into academic achievement should be noted. This is the relation between equality of opportunity and quantity of opportunities to which a student has access. It was shown above that the observed effects of an independent variable relevant for ability and effort on achievement is

$$\frac{a_i}{b} \left[e^{b(t'' - t')} - 1 \right]$$

in the lagged model. If the independent variable is a measure of family background, race, or ethnicity, the effect is commonly taken to be a measure of equality of opportunity. But the observed effect is a function of the opportunities for learning, measured by b. The more opportunities for learning there are, the more inequality of opportunity we will observe, provided that the contribution of the independent variable to a student's ability and effort remains constant over the period t' to t''. Further, given the level of opportunities, we would expect stronger observed effects of background variables the longer the time the process has gone on with the maximum observable effect being $-a_i/b$.

The cross-sectional regression of achievement on background variables will estimate $-a_i/b$ if the cross-section is taken when no more learning takes place. Before then, the cross-sectional model is a misspecification because it omits the lagged term. Observed coefficients would be biased because of the omitted variable, and they would be functions of the amount of time the process had gone on as well as of the opportunities for learning. Despite the misspecification, it is useful to show the cross-sectional results since they are the ones commonly reported. We should here observe more inequality of opportunity among seniors than among sophomores and more inequality of opportunity in academic tracks than in nonacademic tracks. That this is indeed the case can be observed in Table 2, where I present regressions of reading achievement on socioeconomic background and race for the two grade levels.

Although not all of the differences are statistically significant, they are all in the expected direction. Race and socioeconomic background have more of an effect on reading achievement in academic than in nonacademic tracks because the academic tracks provide more opportunities for learning and therefore background has more growth to act on. Similarly, the background variables have stronger effects in the senior than in the sophomore grade because the process has gone on for a longer time for the seniors.

Paradoxically, perhaps, the more students can learn in a school, the more unequal may educational outcomes become

Table 2
Regressions of Reading Achievement on Race and Socioeconomic
Background for Students inTheir Sophomore Year and inTheir
Senior Year in Academic and Nonacademic Tracks

Independent	Academic		Nonacademic	
variables	B	s.e.	B	s.e.
		Seniors		
BYSES	3.974	.529	2.736	.359
RACED	6.080	.959	4.981	.594
Constant	49.577		45.718	
R^2	.161		.117	
N	652		1336	
		Sophomores		
BYSES	2.955	.495	2.637	.363
RACED	5.469	.897	4.122	.551
Constant	47.567		44.334	
R^2	.126		.092	
N	652		1336	

Note: Dependent variable is FYREADSD, reading achievement in senior year. BBREADSD
is reading achievement in sophomore year. BYSES is composite measure of socioeconomic background. RACED is dummy variable for race (white = 1, nonwhite = 0).

by social origins. This, of course, assumes that the relation
between origin and ability and effort persists through schooling. Equality of educational opportunity then can only be
achieved by removing the association between origin and ability. This is perhaps generally recognized. It seems less clearly
recognized that if this association between ability and origin
cannot be removed, then "good" schools, schools where students learn a lot, will, other things being equal, magnify the
observed inequality of opportunity. In addition, I shall show
below that this is not the only matter in which inequality of
educational opportunity is created in schools. In the process of
gaining access to opportunities for learning inequality of opportunity may also be created, and this inequality of opportunity

emerges even if the association between ability and origin is removed.

It is possible to separate variation in opportunities for learning from variation in student characteristics using the proposed model of learning. Also, the important implications of the model for how inequality of opportunity by background depends on the level of opportunities have been supported. The importance of this depends on the manner in which opportunities for learning are allocated to students. This is discussed next.

THE ORGANIZATION OF OPPORTUNITIES FOR LEARNING

Opportunities for learning are not equally available to all students in a school. Students are grouped into instructional groups that vary with respect to their curriculum, teacher effort, and ability. In the primary grades these differences in opportunities for learning are usually (in the United States) produced by within-classroom grouping in the form of ability grouping. At higher grade levels, explicit or informal tracking and other forms of curriculum differentiation provide the differentiation of opportunities.

Schools, at least in the United States, have an ambivalent attitude toward equality of educational outcomes. The comprehensive system of secondary education, or the "common school" (Cremin, 1951), is a unique American institution designed to achieve a basic equality of educational outcome. On the other hand, much educational policy and practice is legitimized by the goal of providing each student the opportunity to develop to the maximum of his potential. The latter will imply maximizing inequality of educational outcomes, since it implies that those with the greater ability should have the more favorable opportunities for learning. Only if no one is provided with more opportunities than the least able can take advantage of will equality of outcome come about. Schools can equalize educational outcome only by equalizing ability and effort, or by teaching very little.

Schools generally make some effort at equalizing ability and effort among students, but much, if not most, of what goes on in schools seems designed to maximize the potential of students by providing the most opportunities for learning to those most able to take advantage of them. For this reason we get, as noted, ability grouping and similar arrangements in the lower grades and often elaborate curriculum differentiation in the higher grades. This has the effect of increasing inequality of educational outcome. It does also, as I shall argue, introduce a source of inequality of opportunity. For the opportunities for learning provided a student never will be only a question of this student's abilities and talents. Opportunities will also be determined by the locale in which students are located—in particular, the characteristics of those students with whom one student competes for access to opportunities for learning. The opportunities for learning will depend on the particular ability groups, classes, tracks, and schools a student attends. This variation in opportunities by locale is not necessarily determined by origins; it is nevertheless a variation in equality of opportunity for learning.

If all instruction in schools were completely individualized, it might be feasible to provide each individual student with the opportunities for learning that are commensurate with the student's ability and effort. But almost all instruction in schools takes place in instructional groups and involves an element of treating all students in the group as though they were alike. Teachers and curricula are assigned to these instructional groups. Hence instructional groups organize opportunities for learning. This is perhaps not very surprising. But the consequence of this is that identical students will in general be provided with different opportunities for learning in different locales. This observation appears to be surprising and its explanation and consequences in need of elaboration, for it is a phenomenon not recognized in much sociological research, although it is a very sociological topic.

The reason why instructional groups structure opportunities for learning in a manner that produces inequality of opportunities among locales is that instructional groups are closed-position systems. By the concept of closed-position system in this context, I mean that instructional groups have an existence quite, though not completely, independent of the characteristics of the students assigned to the groups. It is for this reason that opportunities for learning come to vary independently of student characteristics. The nature of instructional groups as closed-position systems has important consequences for educational processes. It is therefore useful to develop the concept and its consequences further.

Instructional Groups as Closed-Position Systems

The distinction between closed and open positions in social structure goes back to Weber (1968). It refers to the availability of positions in social structure: closed positions are those to which access is restricted, open positions are freely available. In the development of this distinction in the labor market context (Sørensen, 1983) I have used it in a more specific meaning. Here a closed position, or a job, is available only when it is vacant, cither because the previous occupant has left for another position, or because it is a new position. This means that in closed-position systems new allocations of people to positions can take place only when positions become vacant so that the timing of allocations is governed by the timing of the occurrence of vacancies. Further, once a vacancy is filled, it is no longer available to other candidates for the position; allocations of people to positions thus creates interdependencies among the candidates. In contrast, incumbents of positions in open-position systems can be replaced at any moment in time, the occurrence of vacancies is irrelevant for the timing of new allocations, and the allocation of one candidate to a position does not affect the probability that others may obtain the same position.

In labor markets, positions are jobs and the emphasis is on the wages and other job rewards provided by positions.

Open-positions systems are markets with the properties of perfectly competitive markets assumed in standard economic theory. Competition in the market insures that at any moment of time there will be a direct correspondence between the wage level or the position and the productivity of the individual obtaining that wage level. Changes in productivity will immediately be recognized by the market and produce changes in wages and other rewards derived from the labor market.

Closed-position systems of jobs are internal labor markets wherein allocations of people to jobs, and hence wage levels, take place by administrative promotion decisions and not market mechanisms. There is no necessary direct correspondence between the productivity of the incumbent and the wages and other job rewards obtained in the position currently occupied by that individual. Since new matches between people and positions can be established only when new vacancies occur, there is no necessary relationship between the occurrence of such vacancies and whatever changes take place in individual productivity.

In the labor market application, the distinction between open- and closed-position systems is a distinction between two very different ways of matching people with certain characteristics to jobs providing certain levels of job rewards. Applying the same distinction to educational structures is to make a distinction between different mechanisms of matching student to opportunities for learning. An open-position educational system would be one in which some sort of market competition at any moment of time established a direct correspondence between the abilities of students and their opportunities for learning. Since opportunities for learning are associated with instructional groups, this would mean that the organization of instructional groups directly reflected student abilities. It is perhaps difficult to conceive of such systems. It was claimed above that instructional groups tend to be closed-position systems. An elaboration of this claim is instructive.

The conception of educational systems as structures of closed positions is not common; when schools are seen as organizations it is usually as organizations of students, teachers, and administrators. However, places in instructional groups may be seen as elements of social organizations in the same manner as other social organizations. Two types of relations can be defined among instructional groups. One is curriculum relations, linking instructional groups together as it is deemed necessary, to cover some instructional material before some other material (e.g., in a sequence of mathematics) or because different parts of a curriculum should be taught in specific combinations to implement the educational goals of the school. The other form of relations existing among instructional groups is the relation of flows of students created by the movements of students in definite patterns among instructional groups. These flows, of course, often reflect curriculum relationships. They produce explicit or implicit tracks that define educational careers. Elsewhere (Sørensen, 1984) I have shown that these relations can be used to define hierarchies of instructional groups in the same manner as organizational hierarchies in labor market organizations.

The organization of instructional groups gives them an existence that is quite independent of the characteristics of the students that are to fill these groups. There are several reasons for this. First, educational ideologies, as implemented in curriculum requirements imposed by governments and other educational authorities, imply that a minimial set of curriculum units should be formed, regardless of which students attend a particular school. Resources, in the form of teacher availability, set other constraints on the flexibility of a system of instructional groups. Most educational systems, in addition, require that the number of students in instructional groups cannot go above or below certain limits. Not only pedagogical concerns but also the physical layout of school buildings constrain the number of places available in instructional groups. Available equipment provides other constraints. Together, these constraints limit the ability of schools to vary the kinds of instructional groups that may be offered and the number of places in these groups.

Schools then typically will not provide a distribution of places in instructional groups that closely matches the distribution of student characteristics. This proposition may not seem very surprising in the case of between-classroom groupings such as tracks at secondary levels of education. It is perhaps more intriguing that also in the case of within-classroom grouping, such as ability grouping, the size distribution will vary quite independently of the student body from which the groups are formed. Ability groups tend to be few and of equal size, regardless of whether students are highly heterogeneous or highly homogeneous (Hallinan and Sørensen, 1983).

In general, then, there will not be a perfect correspondence between the abilities and interests of students in a particular school and the opportunities for learning that are created by the organization of the instructional groups in that school. This is, however, only one of the conditions for the closed nature of instructional groups. The lack of a match is further reinforced by the existence of important constraints on the mobility between instructional groups. These constraints mean that once a student is assigned to an instructional group, or system of instructional groups such as a track, it is unlikely the student will be reassigned, even if the match between the student's abilities and interests and the opportunities for learning could be improved by a reassignment. Both curriculum differences and organizational arrangements produce these constraints on mobility.

Curriculum relations constrain mobility to the extent that one part of a subject may be a prerequisite for understanding another part of a topic. For example, after students are assigned to ability groups in a classroom, it may be impossible to move a student from a lower group to a higher group because of differences in teaching materials between the groups. These same constraints may apply to movement, particularly in an upward direction, among classes and tracks after they have been formed.

Curriculum differences among instructional groups may not be a reason for the lack of mobility in a downward direction, that is, from an instructional group providing more to one providing fewer opportunities for learning. The lack of extensive downward mobility is prevented simply by the predetermined nature of the size distribution of instructional groups argued above. If the size distribution is to remain intact, any movement out of one group should be compensated by movement into the group. This is in general difficult to achieve as it means that one student's success is to be accompanied by another student's failure.

These organizational constraints on mobility, in between the times when instructional groups are formed, have been documented for within-classroom grouping by Hallinan and Sørensen (1983). In fact, in her qualitative study, Eder (1979) found that teachers would rather reinterpret performance than move students. Rosenbaum (1976) appears to provide a picture of much downward mobility among high school tracks. However, within and between academic year mobility is confounded, and it is in fact more accurate to describe the system as a promotion system wherein more and more students are left without promotion chances as they progress through the systems in a manner similar to how internal labor market systems leave more and more employees without further chances for promotion as they age.

Once assigned to an instructional group and its opportunities for learning, a student then is unlikely to be reassigned. As assignment to one group may be a prerequisite for the assignment to another group, students will be channelled into educational trajectories and mobility between these trajectories will be restricted. The number of places in these trajectories is decided not primarily by ability and interest, although of course this may have some influence, but by curriculum requirements, resources, and architectural consideration. The match between a student's ability and interest and his opportunities for learning is then determined by forces particular to the locale in which the student obtains his education.

The closed nature of instructional groups creates closed educational trajectories so that early assignments become crucial for the educational career. Completely closed educational trajectories run counter to ideology, especially in the United States. Schools may institute a variety of procedures to reduce the inequalities in access to educational opportunities produced by the tendency to a lack of mobility among educational trajectories. It is common to change teachers at every grade level in American schools. Still, the receiving teachers obtain information from former teachers. Eder (1979) reports that first-grade teachers relied heavily on information provided by kindergarten teachers when forming reading groups in the first grade.

The use of elective assignments at secondary educational levels is another device for breaking up the effect of early assignments on later assignments. Nevertheless, the freedom of choice may appear greater than it is in reality. Cicourel and Kitsuse (1963) vividly describe the strong influence, in a high school, that counsellors and teachers have on student choices and show how these choices are manipulated so that available places become filled and the size distribution of instructional groups remains intact.

The closed nature of instructional groups and the educational trajectories they produce not only introduces local variation in the match between student characteristics and opportunities for learning; it also has important implications for the mechanisms by which students are assigned to instructional groups and educational trajectories. I shall show in the next section that the emerging mechanism is one that creates interdependencies among students and influences the choice of criteria for the assignment.

THE ASSIGNMENT TO INSTRUCTIONAL GROUPS

The preceding section argued that the organization of instructional groups defines an opportunity structure students move through as they progress through the educational system. Particular historical and organizational circumstances shape this opportunity structure. Variations among schools in curricula and in the size distributions of instructional groups interact with student-body composition to produce locally specific opportunities for individual students. For example, a student with a

given level of ability may be assigned to a college-bound trajectory in one setting and not in another, simply because the
number of places providing access to higher education differ
in the two settings, despite similar student-body composition.
Because the organization of instructional groups will be largely
independent of the characteristics of the student body, a student's placement in instructional groups becomes dependent
on the particular students with whom he or she is competing.

Table 1 showed that different academic tracks are associated with different opportunities for learning. This finding is
especially important for the creation of inequality of opportunity by the organizational differentiation of students if it indeed
can be shown that tracks have properties of closed-position
systems so that inequality of opportunity is created in the
assignment to tracks. There are two features of closed-position
systems that are especially important for the mechanism that
assigns people to positions. One is the interdependencies among
candidates that lead to the use of rankings in the assignment.
The other is the concern for the prediction of future performance.

By the definition of closed-position systems, new assignments can take place only when vacancies occur. In schools,
this means that places in instructional groups, as argued above,
will usually be filled only at the beginning of the school year,
if not more rarely. When vacancies occur, there will usually be
a well-defined and finite set of them. Also, there will usually
be a well-defined and finite set of candidates for these vacancies. This means that the assignment of one set of candidates
to the vacancies will exclude another set of candidates. A rank-
ing of the candidates will be performed, except when assignments are random.

Schools do perform random assignments, usually between
class groupings with identical curricula at lower grades, and
elective assignments are of importance in American secondary
education. However, nonrandom and nonelective assignments
are, of course, very frequent in assignment to instructional
groups differing in important ways in the opportunities for
learning they provide. Rankings therefore are very frequently

employed in educational decision making, especially those having significance for educational careers.

The interdependencies created by rankings have interesting consequences for competition processes in schools. Ranks have no metric for the distances between ranks and provide no information about these distances. A student may work hard to change his rank order and not achieve the objective because the unmeasurable distance to the next in rank is too great. Rankings also create interdependencies among the efforts of a set of candidates. The display of additional effort by one candidate will provide an incentive for other candidates also to work hard. But if everybody increases their effort, the rank order may remain unchanged. There is therefore an incentive for strategic behavior with the aim of collectively controlling effort since the same outcome will come about if everybody shows little effort as if everybody shows much effort. Peer groups should produce these collective manipulations of efforts, but despite much research on the importance of peer groups for values and aspirations, no research has focused on their importance for controlling effort levels among students.

As argued above, once an assignment is done, it is unlikely to be undone because of the constraints on the mobility between instructional groups and, over longer periods, between educational trajectories. This makes the prediction of future performance an important consideration in the assignment of students to instructional groups differing in opportunities for learning. Any characteristic of students believed to be correlated with performance is potentially usable as an assignment criterion. These characteristics may include ascriptive characteristics such as origin, race, and ethnicity. There is therefore a presumption for inequality of opportunity to emerge in the assignment of students to instructional groups in the manner in which "statistical discrimination" emerges in the labor market. Schools try to avoid this by using past performance to predict future performance and relying on "objective" tests when performing the most important assignments. Though these tests may have stronger metric properties than ordinality, they are inevitably used to produce percentiles so that cutoff points can be established that correspond to the number of available places.

The use of past performance to predict future performance makes assignments to instructional groups differing in opportunities for learning eventually self-fulfilling. This adds to the closed nature of instructional groups and may create strong historical effects on educational careers of individual students. Ability group assignments in the first grade may have consequences for assignments much later in the educational career. Very little is known about these long-term consequences of assignments to instructional groups. We do know (Jackson, 1964) that month of birth correlates with performance on the 11 + examination in Britain because month of birth is important for assignment to ability groups or streams in the first grades: those relatively older (by at most 6 months) when entering first grade have a higher chance of getting into the high groups providing more opportunities for learning.

Empirical Results

A simple example, showing the metric implications of the use of vacancy competition in assignment to ability groups and the importance of the size distribution of groups for the assignment process is available (Sørensen and Hallinan, 1984). Here a simple model for the probability of being assigned to a high group performed significantly better when percentile rank rather than absolute reading achievement level was used as the independent variable. Also, a strong effect of the relative size of the high group was found. This variable in fact removed an effect of race on the probability of being assigned to a high group. Without taking size into account, it appeared that blacks had a higher probability, given their initial reading achievement, of being assigned to a high group. This race effect, it turns out, in this sample of classrooms and schools, simply reflects that black students went to classes where the high group tended to be larger. Except for the different size distributions in black and white schools, the assignment process was similar to schools differing in racial composition.

Similar results can be obtained at the high-school level when focusing on the assignment to academic track. Table 3 presents three models for the assignment to academic track, seen as functions of the student's socioeconomic background, race, achievement, and the size distribution of tracks in the school the student attends.

The first model, presented in the first panel of Table 3, shows that socioeconomic background, achievement, and race are all relevant to whether or not a student will be in the academic track. All three variables are significant. It is noteworthy and perhaps surprising to some that black students have a better chance, other things being equal, of getting into the academic track than white students, according to this model (that

Table 3
Logistic Regressions of Being in Academic Track on Reading Achievement, Race, Socioeconomic Background, and Percentage of Students in Academic Track

Independent variables	Model 1		Model 2		Model 3	
	B	s.e.	B	s.e.	B	s.e.
BBREADSD	.0651	.0048	.0612	.0053		
Z					.6665	.0523
BYSES	.6217	.0633	.3039	.0710	.3709	.0700
RACED	− .1178	.0502	− .0836	.0555	− .0162	.0548
TRACK			.0521	.0027	.0585	.0028
Constant	− 3.8627	.2480	− 5.500	.2983	− 2.7547	.1172
Log likelihood	− 1618.630		− 1366.166		− 1348.348	

Note: Dependent variable is probability of being in academic track in sophomore year. TRACK is the percentage of students in academic track in respondents schools. Z is the z score for respondent give the mean and standard deviation of reading achievement for his school. BBREADSD is reading achievement in sophomore year. BYSES is composite measure of socioeconomic background. RACED is dummy variable for race (white = 1, nonwhite = 0).

conceptually is similar to other models reported in the literature on track assignment).

The second model presented in Table 3 shows that the relative size of the academic track is a significant variable for the assignment to academic track. The larger the relative size of the academic track, the more likely it is that a student will be assigned to this educational trajectory, providing, as we have shown above, better opportunities for learning. Once demonstrated, this is perhaps not so very surprising. However, the result confirms a major point argued above: schools structure educational opportunities in a manner quite independent of the characteristics of the students assigned to these opportunities. The introduction of this school characteristic does have relevance for our inferences regarding the relevance of student characteristics for the assignment process. The introduction of the relative size of academic track almost removes the effect of race on the assignment. The main reason why blacks have a better chance of getting into the academic track is that schools attended by blacks have larger academic tracks than schools attended by whites, given the characteristics of their students.

The third model of Table 3 now demonstrates that, as argued above, it will be the relative standing of the individual student among his peers that will be decisive for the assignment. The variable Z is the z score of the individual student's measured achievement, given the mean for the school he attends and the variance for that school. This change of metric reduces the log likelihood considerably with the same number of independent variables. The improvement in fit is obtained by measuring a main determinant of the outcome of the assignment in a manner consistent with the vacancy competition process argued to be operative in closed-position systems and its use of rankings.

These results are parallel to those reported in Sørensen and Hallinan (1984) for the assignment to ability groups in primary grades. Together these results provide evidence for a pervasive mechanism of allocation of students to instructional groups differing in opportunities for learning throughout the schooling process.

CONCLUSION

Opportunities for learning determine how much a student will learn. The more opportunities presented, the more strongly will a student's ability affect measured educational outcomes. To the extent that background characteristics continue to be related to students' abilities to take advantage of the opportunities for learning, more opportunity will produce more inequality of opportunity. The analysis of the impact of the different opportunities for learning in academic and in other tracks in high school demonstrates this.

Schools do not affect observed inequality of educational outcomes only by providing different overall levels of opportunities for learning. They also structure these opportunities differently in different locales. Hence individual students will be provided different opportunities depending on where they go to school. Because of the local determination of opportunities for learning, a student's access to the opportunities provided will depend on whom he competes with for access to these opportunities.

Educational attainment processes are far more contingent on local conditions than sociological research on educational attainment processes would lead one to believe. The reason we ignore it is that most research appears to have ignored the variables that create these contingencies and has used models for the measurement of school effects that cannot detect these contingencies. Research that incorporates the ideas advocated here may perhaps make future research on these issues a bit more realistic and sociologically interesting.

Acknowledgments

The superb research assistance of Jutta Allmendinger is gratefully acknowledged.

REFERENCES

Cicourel, Aaron V. and John I. Kitsuse. 1963. *The Educational Decision Makers*. Indianapolis: Bobbs-Merrill.

Coleman, James S. 1968. "The mathematical study of change." Pp. 428–478 in Herbert M. Blalock and A. B. Blalock (eds.), *Methodology in Social Research*. New York: McGraw-Hill.

Coleman, James S., Ernest Q. Campbell, Carol J. Hobson, James McPartland, Alexander M. Mood, Frederic D. Weinfeld. and Robert L. York. 1966. *Equality of Educational Opportunity*. Washington, D.C.: U.S. Government Printing Office.

Coleman, James S., Thomas Hoffer, Sally Kilgore. 1982. *High School Achievement*. New York: Basic Books.

Cremin, Laurence A. 1951. *The American Common School*. New York: Knopf.

Eder, Donna J. 1979. *Stratification Within the Classroom: The Formation and Maintenance of Ability groups*. Unpublished dissertation, University of Wisconsin—Madison.

Hallinan, Maureen T. and Aage B. Sørensen. 1983. "The formation and stability of instructional groups." *American Sociological Review* 48:838–51.

Jackson, Brian. 1964. *Streaming*. London: Routledge and Kegan Paul.

Rosenbaum, James E. 1976. *Making Inequality*. New York: Wiley.

Sørensen, Aage B. 1983. "Processes of allocation to closed and open positions in social structure." *Zeitschrift für Soziologie* 12:203–24.

Sørensen, Aage B. 1984. "The organizational differentiation of students in schools." Pp. 25–44 in Hans Oosthoek and Pieter van den Eeden (eds.), *Education from the Multilevel Perspective: Models, Methodology and Empirical Findings*. London: Gordon and Breach.

Sørensen, Aage B. and Maureen T. Hallinan. 1978. "A reconceptualization of school effects." *Sociology of Education* 50:273–289.

Sørensen, Aage B. and Maureen T. Hallinan. 1984. "Effect of race on the assignment to ability groups." Pp. 85–103 in Penelope Peterson, Louise C. Wilkinson, and Maureen T. Hallinan (eds.), *The Social Context of Instruction*. New York: Academic Press.

Sørensen, Aage B. and Maureen T. Hallinan. 1986. "Effects of ability grouping on growth in academic achievement." *American Educational Research Journal*.

Weber, Max. 1968. *Economy and Society*. Berkeley: University of California Press.

CHAPTER 6

Evaluating the Trade-offs in Student Outcomes from Alternative School Organization Policies

JAMES M. McPARTLAND and ROBERT L. CRAIN

At a few key points in the history of American public schools, tensions have surfaced between the goal of educational equity—providing egalitarian access to all levels of education—and the goal of educational quality—maintaining high standards of student performance. These occasions include the debate over a common curriculum prompted by the report of the Committee of Ten in 1893, the emergence of vocational course offerings that accompanied the 1918 NEA Commission's "Cardinal Principles of Secondary Education," and curriculum proposals to improve the comprehensive high school and upgrade instruction in mathematics and science beginning in the 1950s following the Conant reports and in reaction to Sputnik. But usually

James M. McPartland • Center for Social Organization of Schools, Johns Hopkins University, Baltimore, MD 21218.   Robert L. Crain • Teachers College, Columbia University, New York, NY 10027.

Americans ignore dilemmas between equity and quality in their debates about school policy, apparently assuming that schools can progress on both fronts without making trade-offs between them and without making difficult decisions about resource allocations and cost efficiencies.

We are again at a point of tension. Public attention to educational policy has been enlivened by a recent combination of influential reports and a sense of international competition. Education policy makers often find it difficult to lead a public discussion of equity versus quality dilemmas. But this discussion must be conducted; therefore education researchers must consider current school reform proposals in terms of the tensions between goals of equity and quality. In particular, we need (a) clear substantive discussions of why trade-offs may arise (specifying the processes and social mechanisms whereby progress on one goal threatens progress on the other) and (b) empirical research to evaluate the extent of the dilemmas under alternative school policies and practices. In other words, we must understand more fully when equity–quality dilemmas may actually arise and develop the knowledge required to design governmental programs and/or regulations that can achieve balance when the goals are in competition (Astin, 1982, Okun, 1975).

This chapter examines three major policy components of current reform proposals that appear particularly prone to the tensions between equity and quality. These areas are (1) tests and standards for promotion or graduation, (2) common or differentiated curriculum, and (3) choice of schools and programs. Research issues in the sociology of education related to these tensions will be discussed.

THE CONCEPTS OF EDUCATIONAL QUALITY AND EQUITY

Generally, when people discuss the tension between goals of educational quality (or educational excellence) and educational equity (or equality of educational opportunity), they are concerned with changes in the average and distribution of important student outcomes and with access of different segments of the population to different levels of schooling. Concern with educational quality goals arise when there is evidence that the *average* performance on some important student outcome (like a mathematics test) is lower than at some earlier period or in comparison to some other jurisdiction or nation. Concern with educational quality goals also often focuses on the *top* segment of the distribution of student outcome scores: are the schools producing as many students with outstanding performances compared to earlier times or to other school systems?

On the other hand, concerns with educational equity goals usually reflect interest in the proportion of different social groups that are enrolled as students at different education levels and how the performance of students at the *lower* end of the distribution compares to others on important learning outcomes. Thus, a school system would be judged to be more successful in achieving equity goals when it enrolls a higher proportion of all segments of the student-aged population and when the "gap" between the highest-achieving and lowest-achieving students is smaller. This achievement gap could be viewed in several ways, as the spread of achievement at a given point in time, or the relative growth rates over time by students with different starting points, or the relationship of student performance with family background or social class measures.

Several statistical measures have been developed for examination of the comparative quality of a school system and of achievement gaps related to educational equity concepts. International studies have examined growth in average test score achievement from ages 10 to 14 to measure quality, and changes in dispersion (standard deviation) of achievement to measure equality (Coleman, 1985). Klitgaard (1973) has discussed interpretations of a number of statistical indicators of the distribution of student outcome scores. Some of these deal with school impacts on equalizing student performance or increasing mobility, others with the comparative school effects for the most advantaged and most disadvantaged students, and others with producing certain minimum achievements for all students. These statistics include measures of spread (such as the standard deviation or interquartile range), indicators of distortions in the distribution (such as skewness), and proportions of students below a specific achievement score. Other economists and sociologists have developed measures to tap changes in inequalities of income distributions (Allison, 1978; Schwartz and Winship, 1980) that might be applied to educational outcome data (Baker and McPartland, 1982).

Another concept closely related to some notions of educational equity is Edmonds's (1979) definition of "the effective school" as the school that reduces or even eliminates the correlation between students' family background and academic achievement. Statistical interaction measures that follow from this definition have been used in empirical studies of school effects (Hauser, Sewell, and Alwin, 1976) and for comparisons between public and private high schools (Greeley, 1982; McPartland and McDill, 1982).

Conditions for Goal Conflict

Various definitions of the goals of educational quality and equity produce different images of the extent and source of conflict between them. The potential for conflict between these goals is clearest when the resources for education are limited and the pursuit of one goal does not contribute to the achievement of the other. In this case, the problem by definition is that the resources invested in the pursuit of one goal will take away from investments in reaching for the other goal. But other definitions of the two goals can complicate the matter. For example, the degree of incompatibility of goals might be quite different under three different definitions of equity of resource allocation: students' need for schooling versus students' ability to benefit from further schooling versus students' likelihood of putting further schooling to profitable use (Strike, 1985). Also, the simple definition of equity as the equal distribution of the *same* educational resources across all population groups has been confronted by alternative conceptions of equal educational opportunities that consider how students may differ in their responsiveness to particular changes in school resources (Coleman, 1968).

To appreciate how complex it can become to estimate equitable distribution of educational resources, consider how access to microcomputers in education has been discussed in terms of equity and differences in student needs (Becker, 1985). Is it inequality when low-achieving students receive drill and practice on computers in basic skills where their need is great while high achievers who have mastered the basic skills use their computer access time to practice computer programming? If we say that it is not inequitable for high achievers and low achievers to use the computer differently, then we imply that it may also not be inequitable for the low achievers to receive more microcomputer resources, because the amount of access time needed for drill and practice to improve basic skills may be much larger than the access time needed to develop programming skills. The example of computer use suggests that instructional practice may vary without being inequitable if a better match is achieved to meet different student needs and that precise determinations of equitable distributions will not be easy.

But as a matter of public education policy, the tension between equity and quality goals is most often contained in the question of whether a democratic (mass) educational system that enrolls high proportions of all segments of society can produce the same levels of student performances—especially at the upper end of the distribution—as would be achieved by an educational system that was more selective (elite). When attention turns from achievement test performance to the utility of different amounts and type of schooling for the next stages of life, such as continuation in education and success in adult occupations, the type of school curriculum that is most useful for one purpose may not be as useful for other purposes. In most European countries and in Japan, the distinction between preparation for advanced education versus training for employment is reflected in a two-tiered system of differentiated schools

(Husen, 1979; James and Benjamin, 1984; Max Planck Institute, 1983; Moody, 1978; Silver, 1973). One tier is for university-bound students, with selective entrance requirements. The other tier, for all others, emphasizes technical skills and terminates more quickly. But all of these modern industrial states have had serious political debates about whether the degree and timing of selectivity of their educational systems was striking the proper balance between goals of quality and equity for their nations.

In our country, recent policy proposals regarding school requirements, curriculum, and access are directly related to the potential conflicts between goals or educational quality and equity, although our public debates do not highlight this relationship. We will consider each set of proposals to discuss why it is plausible to expect trade-offs between the two goals to be at issue and to suggest research information that can help evaluate the dilemmas and alternatives.

TESTS AND STANDARDS FOR PROMOTION OR GRADUATION

Unlike many European countries, American school systems have seldom established formal system-level tests or examinations to qualify students for entry and continuation in programs or for certification at the completion of a program (the Regents Examinations in New York state tied to differentiated high-school diplomas is an exception). Until recently, decisions to promote students to the next grade were made at the local school-building level on the basis of evaluation and standards established by individual teachers or building officials, and nonpromotion had become a rare event in most public schools. Also, diplomas for high-school graduation had been awarded primarily on the basis of attendance and the completion of sufficient courses with passing grades, with course evaluations made by individual teachers on idiosyncratic measures rather than with system-wide tests. Many localities, responding to political pressures, permitted social promotion and graduations with minimal regard for a student's academic merit or accomplishments.

The late 1970s and 1980s, however, saw the introduction of state and school-district minimum competency examinations (Austin and Garber, 1982; Jaeger, 1982; Schwartz, 1984). These tests, now mandated in at least 40 states, are usually given at both the elementary and secondary levels and are frequently tied to promotion to the next level of schooling or to the award of a high-school diploma (Resnick and Resnick, 1985, p. 14). These tests are now developed and adopted by local or state-wide education agencies, but public opinion polls indicate that most of the American public supports a national high-school graduation test (Elam, 1978), and state education officials are organizing to propose common achievement measures for better state-by-state performance comparisons. Suggestions have also been made to expand the tests currently in use by states and school districts beyond "minimimum competence" to have them assess additional levels of performance that could be tied to differentiated sets of diplomas or certificates.

The potential quality–equity dilemma arises from (a) the standard or level of competence that is set by school officials and (b) the consequences for students who fail to achieve the standard. Different decisions on either of these elements can bring potential costs or benefits to students at either extreme of the achievement distributions.

The theory that higher official standards for performance will improve educational quality assumes that certain motivational and instructional processes will follow the standards. When important consequences for students are tied to evaluations of whether they meet the new standard, students are expected to put forth special effort to pass the evaluation. Thus, higher standards should serve to motivate increased effort by students who wish to receive the benefits of passing and avoid the penalties of failure. Of course, how much effort particular students require to meet the standard will depend upon how near or far their current levels of performance are from the cutoff point tied to the desired outcomes. The same absolute standard that sets a reasonable goal to encourage the striving of some students will offer little or no motivation for students who either are so far below the required level that it is beyond their reach or have already mastered the competencies and can pass the criteria with no additional effort.

It is also expected that new official educational standards will affect classroom instruction directly as teachers gear their classwork assignments and their expectations for student learning to meet these external standards (Popham *et al.*, 1985). Again, the level at which the standard is set will have different effects on the quality of instruction for students at various points on the distribution of current performance. If the absolute standard is low, as in most minimum competency tests, teaching may become aimed at the tested minimum and reduce the instructional quality of the program for students at the top end of the distribution. Thus, students at the low end may benefit from an instructional concentration on these competencies, but students who already have mastered such skills will not be exposed to the challenging classroom demands and instruction they may otherwise have received. These concerns about the "curricular reductionism" that follows from setting low-level standards have been recognized by others, and there are claims that teachers attend so much to the elements of minimum competency tests that instructional standards and practices are *lower* for all but the weakest students (Resnick and Resnick, 1985).

Where the standard is set will also affect the percentage of students who fail. Indeed, cutoff points on tests are determined in part by estimating what percentage will fail and whether that percentage is administratively acceptable (Sheppard, 1983). Thus, setting a standard well above the minimum competencies now used in many states may induce an instructional program that meets the needs of more students, but at the same time it may generate a higher percentage of students who fail to pass the standard.

Whether an increased percentage of failures is a cost or a benefit to the students who fall below the standard depends upon what actions follow from the failure. If new higher standards are used only to select which students will qualify for a credential or for entry into the next level of education, and those who fail to qualify are excluded from the system, a serious negative personal consequence has been created for those who are so excluded (Howe, 1984; Toch, 1984). This is especially true in an economy with limited employment opportunities for youth, where those who leave school before graduating from high school have a poor chance to substitute useful employment experience during this period. Thus, when a student as a result of a new standard is denied a high-school diploma that would have provided access to certain jobs or further education, we have an example of the trade-off between quality and equity: the diploma based on new standards may be worth more to those who qualify, but those who do not qualify lose access to valuable outcomes.

The negative impacts on students at the bottom end of the performance distribution may also be indirect. Failure to meet new standards in earlier grades and the consequences that flow from such failures may lead to added frustration and alienation from school for some students and increase their probability of dropping out before receiving the high-school diploma (McDill, Natriello, and Pallas, 1986).

On the other hand, students who initially fall below new standards may benefit if educational resources are reallocated to effective programs of corrective or remedial instruction to bring them up to standard and prepare them for the next stage of schooling. Such a corrective instruction approach has been advocated in theories of "mastery learning," where evaluations to identify individuals who are not yet able to meet specific criteria in an instructional sequence are used to provide them with corrective instruction to meet the criteria and move on to the next learning goals (Block and Burns, 1976). Viewed in this way, competency tests would be used as "diagnostic" devices to identify students who need to receive extra instructional resources. Some states and localities have recently modified their resource allocation formulas to direct additional assistance for remediation to schools that show low student performance on mandated competency tests.

COMMON OR DIFFERENTIATED CURRICULUM

The issue of curriculum offerings and requirements has arisen several times in the history of American debates of school policy and each time has drawn some attention to tensions between equality and quality. In simplest terms, the issue is the extent to which there should be a common core curriculum for all students rather than a differentiated program of alternative offerings to meet a diversity of student interests, needs, and abilities. From the earliest days of public education in this country, the notion was developed of a common school that enrolled all segments of the community in the same school building with the same core curriculum of subjects (Cremin, 1951). A powerful egalitarian ideology has historically influenced decisions to minimize and postpone the specialization of curriculum and selectivity of admissions in American public schools. In fact, each time the American school system has extended admission to greater proportions of the population, a much more highly differentiated educational structure has developed than the founding ideologies would suggest (Nasaw, 1979). Often the differentiation has been within schools, as different programs, tracks, subject offerings, and instructional ability groupings are defined (Fenstermacher and Goodlad, 1983).

The belief that this differentiation of educational offerings has reduced the overall quality of American schools has led to some recent reform recommendations. Many of the recent reports on school reform have called for upgrading the minimum course requirements for all students, including the minimum number of courses in major subjects (such as English, math, science, and foreign languages) that would be necessary to earn a high-school diploma (Adler, 1983; Boyer, 1983; National Commission on Excellence in Education, 1983; Sizer, 1984). These reports have argued that a core curriculum going beyond minimum levels should be mandated for all students regardless of whether they plan to continue their education after high school or enter the work force.

The costs and benefits to students of common core curricula or differentiated curricula depend upon whether we are considering high- or low-achieving students and upon how we view the homogeneity or heterogeneity of student instructional groupings as a factor in the learning environment. The common curriculum has potential costs for both high- and low-achieving student groups because each group will have special interests, needs, or abilities that may not be well met by a common curriculum (Coleman, 1981). But the social mechanisms at work in differentiated curricula appear to create greater costs or risks primarily for the lower-achieving students.

The potential costs of a common curriculum to the top students would be generated by a watered-down program designed for the average student in the school. This program would neither offer the instructional coverage nor make the performance demands that would encourage optimum learning on the part of the most able students. Depending upon how the student enrollment is determined in classes of a common core program, the top students run the risk that the level of instruction and the expectations or standards for performance will not stimulate and challenge them as would the offerings and demands of a differentiated selective curriculum.

Similarly, there are potential costs of a common curriculum to low-achieving students. Secondary-school students who are unlikely to continue their education beyond high school may be deprived of the instruction that would prove most useful in the job market and exposed instead to a common curriculum that focuses on academic content designed as prerequisite for college. Moreover, the holding power of the secondary school may be much weaker for non-college-bound students in a common curriculum than in a differentiated curriculum better matched to their needs and interests. In the earlier grades as well a differentiated curriculum may be more highly motivating and instructionally effective for low-achieving students when the course content and level of competition are more closely matched to their prior academic preparation.

On the other hand, the potential academic costs of a differentiated curriculum appear to be negligible for high-achieving students who would follow a high-level exclusive curriculum[1] but very serious for students at the lower extremes, who would wind up in the lower or less-selective tracks. These costs include exposure to instructional programs with poorer resources or weaker educational climates and foreclosure of access to later educational opportunities. Each of these costs can arise from quite different processes.

Lower, less selective tracks are more likely to have poorer instructional resources, because powerful social forces often direct the allocation of better instructional resources to upper-level tracks or programs at the expense of the lower levels. The more academically able students are more likely to come from middle- and upper-class families who have more time and power to influence resource allocation decisions politically. More selective upper-level programs are also likely to be viewed by teachers and school officials as prestigious or rewarding to teach, and these programs may be offered as a reward to the best teachers or will otherwise draw the strongest instructional staff. Recent tabulations of the *High School and Beyond* survey data show that over one-quarter of high-school principals offer assignment to teach the better students as a reward to their instructional staff. Thus, without some explicit policy to allocate instructional resources otherwise, separation of students into differentiated programs will often be accompanied by funding and staffing decisions that provide the selective upper-level programs with better instructional resources.

In addition, the educational climate is often less demanding and less well focused on learning activities in the lower-level tracks and programs (Goodlad, 1983; Heyns, 1978). Low

[1]However, nonacademic outcomes may be a different matter; school desegregation research indicates that adult abilities to function well in ethnically mixed settings are better developed in students of both races who have attended ethnically mixed schools (Braddock, Crain, and McPartland, 1984).

teacher expectations for students in these classes place few demands on students for learning, and students internalize the belief that they cannot become academically capable. Instruction in lower-level tracks is also likely to cover less material and to offer fewer challenges when the teacher aims the lessons at the average student in the class, because this "steering group" average will be a lower standard than that established in the higher-track classes. Teachers are also likely to spend more time enforcing student discipline and less time on academics in lower-track classes.

Students coming from lower-track classes will often be closed off from later educational opportunities because they will not have completed the formal prerequisites for admission to the next educational stages. For example, students in a vocational program that offers job-oriented courses in place of the course units required for most college admissions are foregoing their chances for a later college education. The same effects may occur indirectly if lower-track students are given watered-down versions of courses required for college and thus fail to attain the skills they would need later to sustain a college program.

CHOICE OF OR ASSIGNMENT TO SCHOOLS

A variety of proposals have been offered in recent years to increase parents' choice of their child's school and to introduce market mechanisms into the allocation of resources to individual schools. These proposals would provide educational vouchers to families with school-age children, give tuition tax credits to users of private schools, or establishing open enrollment plans or magnet school programs to attract voluntary school enrollments within or across districts (Coleman, 1980; Doyle and Levine, 1984; Salganik, 1981). At various times, both educational quality and educational equity considerations have been used to argue for and against these proposals.

Although many of the arguments about parental choice in education are ideological ones about the proper role of government, many favor or oppose particular choice proposals on the basis of the effects they expect on educational quality or equity. Proponents predict that choice proposals will improve the quality of schools in several ways. First, under the competition and market mechanisms generated by certain voucher proposals, the poorly run schools will no longer attract students and more effective schools will replace them as favorites of parental choice. Second, parental choices should produce a better match between individual students' learning styles or needs and the appropriate educational environment, especially as more diverse sets of alternative schools develop. Third, schools that enroll students who are there by choice rather than by assignment should more easily develop a positive educational climate and effectively establish higher demands, because students will be more committed to the school. Fourth, educational choice should produce schools that have more homogeneous enrollments in terms of student values and talents, which may improve the learning environments for the most talented students because they will no longer be held back by a school that enrolls a wide range of student abilities.

Proponents of choice proposals also expect positive effects on educational equity, for several reasons. First, they argue that choice programs will provide quality educational alternatives to a wider segment of the population, especially to students now attending the weakest schools in the poorest districts. The only families who presently have educational choices are those who can afford to move to residential locations that have strong public schools or to send their children to private schools. Second, some proponents believe that certain voucher proposals will enhance educational opportunities more than other methods for directly improving the education of minority and disadvantaged students—such as revised state education finance formulas to distribute more resources to poor districts, or local school system actions to terminate poor teachers, attract more good teachers, and upgrade instruction in schools serving the poor. They see these finance reforms and school improvement approaches for educational equity as coming up against entrenched interests in wealthy subdivisions, teacher unions, and school bureaucracies that can be effectively circumvented through the market mechanisms of parental choice. In effect, these critics believe that the best way for the poor to improve their childrens' education is to be freed from a public system that is not capable of significantly improving itself.

The opponents of choice proposals are usually most concerned about threats to equal educational opportunities, and they doubt that extra regulations, provisions, or incentives to accompany any new educational choice policies will offset these threats. Some believe that any improvements in school quality created by increasing parental choice will benefit middle- and upper-class families more than disadvantaged families. They predict that choice policies will create schools with more homogeneous student enrollments, but students from disadvantaged backgrounds would benefit most from a heterogenous student context that included a wide range of student backgrounds. And they feel that there will always be a clear hierarchy of schools along a single dimension of quality for most families, which means that some *selectivity* criteria for admissions will be imposed. Many advocates of educational vouchers understand this concern and promise admission rules (such as random lotteries or first-come, first-served) that do not allow elitist or segregated schools (Coons and Sugarman, 1977, 1981; Greeley, 1977). Those who are concerned about equity effects suspect that the politically powerful will sooner or later influence the selectivity rules so that they do actually sort on social class and race.

RESEARCH TO INFORM EQUITY–QUALITY ISSUES

Three kinds of research can contribute to debates on the equity–quality dilemmas raised by the three education policy questions we have been discussing. First, *traditional* research areas in the sociology of education that are concerned with the effects of how students are grouped for instruction are central to each of the policy questions. Second, *applied* education research that examines alternative remedial schooling efforts can inform discussions of practical policy alternatives. Third, *new* research directions are called for that examine the effects of external factors such as governmental education policy on school practice.

Research on Grouping Practices

We have discussed the fact that many of the equity–quality questions flowing from recent educational reform proposals concern the grouping of students in schools and classrooms. Each policy area—standards, curriculum, and choice—can produce revised instructional groupings in schools, programs, tracks, or classes. New promotion and graduation standards could be used to differentiate students at earlier grades into more homogeneous groups based on current academic achievement. New curriculum requirements could produce either more heterogeneous or more homogeneous student groupings, depending upon whether separate sections by student achievement level are defined for courses with similar curriculum content but different difficulty levels. Choices by students and parents to schools or programs could produce student instructional groupings that are more homogeneous on values, needs or abilities, or family background characteristics, depending upon selectivity and admissions criteria. Thus, in each case, the basic research question of which students benefit most from different degrees of homogeneity or heterogeneity of instructional groupings is at the center of the equity–quality issue.

Effects of different student grouping practices have been extensively studied by sociology of education and educational psychology researchers. They have examined ability grouping in the elementary grades (Slavin, 1986), tracking in the secondary grades (Alexander and Cook, 1982), and the effects of school desegregation on student achievement (Crain and

Mahard, 1983). This body of work has been plagued by a major research problem: separating factors of self-selection and individual differences that precede assignment of instructional groups from the direct effects of the homogeneous versus heterogeneous grouping on student development. As a consequence, although we know much about how students are assigned to different instructional groups and how the groups differ in classroom processes (Peterson, Wilkinson, and Hallinan, 1984), we know much less about which effects on student learning come from different grouping practices.

Basic research on grouping practices in education will be most valuable to equity–quality issues if we can solve the research design problems to get clearer evidence about effects on student learning. In particular, we need studies of the effects of different versions of homogeneous and heterogeneous grouping, including comparisons of between-class and within-class group practices, contrasts of different ranges of student achievement mixes in particular grades and subjects, and evaluations of programs that use heterogeneous grouping for some subjects and homogeneous grouping for other subjects in the same grade. Such basic research on effects of grouping alternatives will be immediately useful for judging the equity–quality potential of school reforms that produce clear changes in how students are grouped for instruction.

Research on Remediation

We have discussed why the efficacy of remedial instruction is a key issue in evaluating the equity–quality issues of policies that use new tests and standards for promotion or graduation. These policies can benefit educational equity if they are combined with effective diagnostic and remedial programs for students who fall behind. Thus, we need research that provides clear evidence about cost-effective approaches to remediation.

We need studies of the costs and effects of new corrective instruction programs that might accompany new testing policies to reduce most negative student consequences. Remedial approaches for low-achieving students could include retaining them in grade for an additional term, requiring summer school, assigning a higher proportion of time for basic skills each day (replacing other activities), setting up "pull-out" courses with remedial specialist teachers, providing after-school tutorial programs, providing Saturday school, and organizing daily corrective instruction within a student's own classroom. These approaches can employ various instructional materials, methods, and delivery systems. Some instructional approaches will be costly (e.g., regular individualized tutorial instruction with a trained remedial specialist); therefore cost-efficiency issues must be considered in designing remediation programs.

Previous evaluations of alternative remedial programs are of little help. The poor quality of existing evidence is suggested by the literature reviews of grade-retention studies (Holmes and Matthews, 1984; Jackson, 1975; Johnson, 1984), which are symptomatic of the shortcomings of present research on other alternative approaches to remediation. But the research does imply, in general, that low-achieving students will respond to extra learning resources with significant added growth in achievement. The potential impact of remedial programs is suggested by research indicating that students from low-income families fall behind others in learning mostly during the summer months but stay even during the school term (Heyns, 1978) and by studies that find considerable extra learning by students who remain in school compared to students with similar abilities who drop out or fail to continue their education (Alexander, Natriello, and Pallas, 1985). These results imply that adding more school learning time during the summer and during the regular school term for students who are behind would be one way to close the achievement gaps. But we do not know at what grades remedial instruction will work best and what remedial approaches will be most cost-effective. Preliminary evidence shows the promise of the "promotional gates" program in New York city schools, which retains low-achieving students at grades 4 and 7 but provides them with summer instruction followed by yearlong remedial classes that have greatly reduced teacher–student ratios and added instructional resources (Frank, 1984).

Studies from other compensatory education projects provide no clear guidelines for what will work best (Rhine, 1981) but suggest that remedial programs should be carefully coordinated with regular classroom instruction to be most beneficial and to eliminate the possibilities that pull-out students may be overlooked in their regular classes and given inappropriate lessons in their special classes. We need extensive new research that evaluates the cost efficiency of different categories of remedial education for students who have fallen behind at different grade levels in order to clarify the kinds of educational investments that will be required to maintain equity goals as new quality standards for promotion and graduation are implemented.

Research on External School Policies

With the possible exceptions of studies that link changes in college entrance requirements to changes in elementary and secondary school curriculum (e.g., Coleman, 1985) and research on the "white flight" that sometimes follows school desegregation court orders (Rossell, 1985), little past research has examined how schools change in the face of changes in their external environments. Because some versions of proposed reforms in promotion and graduation standards are now in place or may be soon, we will be able to evaluate directly their impact on school practice. But since we do not yet have local natural variations of the proposed reforms in choice of schools we will have to locate analogous situations in other segments of our educational system or in other countries in order to find empirical evidence on the likely outcomes.

Changes in Promotion or Graduation Standards: Studies of Direct Variation. Reforms have been adopted by many state agencies and local districts to institute testing programs that are tied to promotion or graduation standards. In most cases, minimum competency scores are established for promotion or graduation. We now need careful study of how setting these new standards affects teacher, school, and student practices in order to learn what changes in instructional content and motivation flow from specific modifications in testing programs and policies.

Studies of the effects of setting new standards at different levels of difficulty are needed to assess the equity–quality dilemmas. Studies of changes in actual classroom practice that follow from instituting new minimum competency requirements are needed to test the theory that weaker students will benefit at the expense of stronger students due to changes in teacher expectations and instruction aimed at these minimums. Comparisons of how students respond to new standards set at varying higher levels, including changes in student learning as well as changes in student alienation and withdrawal, are needed to evaluate the true positive or negative impacts experienced by students who begin at different points on the achievement distribution.

Choice and Selectivity in Education: Studies of Analogous Situations. Proposed reforms for educational choice of schools have not been implemented in this country except in a few special cases; we must find indirect ways to bring empirical evidence to the key questions. The major equity–quality questions involve the effects of educational choice proposals on the selectivity and homogeneity of schools. Following public policies to increase parental choice as the basis for student assignment to schools, what effect can be expected on the selectivity and homogeneity of school enrollments? Will the resulting system produce a greater homogeneity of enrollments within schools and a greater heterogeneity between schools? What attributes of family background, family values, and student needs or abilities will be involved in the changes in school selectivity and homogeneity?

To examine these questions indirectly, we suggest a closer study of state variations at the postsecondary level. Our system of higher education provides significant student choice, has strong public and private sectors in many states, and includes a differentiated system of two-year and four-year institutions that uses different selection criteria in different localities. Through careful comparisons of different states' postsecondary systems and direct studies of changes in particular state postsecondary policies we should be able to learn a good deal about which policies create the most homogeneous and segregated enrollments on various student attributes and which state policies produce programs of high quality by different measures.

State contrasts should show which specific regulations on the location of program offerings and criteria for admission selectivity can minimize class and race segregation while permitting other useful choice differentiations. State comparisons of social group differences in college completion rates and in other college productivity and quality measures, such as continuation to postgraduate study in selective programs, should also increase our understanding of the potential equity–quality effects of educational choice under different incentives and constraints.

In using research from the postsecondary level in our states to inform policy questions about increasing choice at the elementary and secondary levels, we will have to clarify how well the analogy fits between the levels to interpret any emerging findings. Just as international comparisons of school policies that keep unique national factors in mind can provide very useful direct evidence on new education proposals in this country, we believe careful comparisons of state postsecondary systems will provide analogous evidence on the likely equity and quality consequences of alternative educational choice policies.

SUMMARY

Questions about the degree of incompatibility between goals of educational quality and equity must be addressed in a more analytic way than has usually been the case in American debates about educational policy and practice. We must understand when policy alternatives involve real trade-offs so that the political process can properly and effectively address the value conflicts or questions of priority that are raised. We also need knowledge of how effective various policies may be in reducing these dilemmas—policies such as public regulations to constrain behavior, public incentives to attract desired individual actions, or public investments to compensate for unintended negative outcomes. Our goal in this chapter has been to examine the potential quality–equity tensions that underly three current educational policy topics and to suggest reseach to help clarify the trade-offs of proposed policy alternatives under each topic. We examined the equity–quality issue mainly in terms of whether students at the top or bottom of the achievement distribution benefit or lose from the proposed reform.

Who benefits and who loses from different decisions to use new tests or standards for students at key passage points in elementary and secondary grades obviously depends upon where the cutting point is made and what consequences follow from falling below the standard. To the extent that instructional resources will be directed to skills needed to pass the standard, the quality of education should improve for students who do not yet have the skills and can be taught them under the usual terms of instruction. Thus, minimum competency tests may benefit students at the bottom of the performance distribution at the expense of other students who have already mastered the requisite skills. Failure to pass the standard, wherever it is placed, can have either positive or negative consequences, depending upon whether failing students are excluded from access to valuable further education or admitted to remedial instruction that addresses their needs with additional resources. We call for research both to assess the impact on classroom practice of new tests or standards and to identify the cost effectiveness of alternative remediation approaches.

Who benefits and who loses from establishing a common curriculum depends both upon the value of the new curriculum content and upon the extent to which students will be separated into more homogeneous achievement groups within the common content areas. Because homogeneous grouping for instruction is now frequently used in American education, it is not easy to predict what changes in the extent and frequency of ability grouping by student achievement will result from adopting specific proposals for curriculum changes. We call for basic research to evaluate more clearly the learning consequences of different grouping arrangements for students at different grades and achievement levels.

Who benefits and who loses from policies to introduce market mechanisms for increasing choice of schools also depends upon considerations of instructional content and the instructional groupings of students that are likely to follow from the selectivity practices that must accompany greater choice. We view predictions on these matters to be part of a broad new research area that relates changes in the external environment to changes in school practice. Because actual comparisons of many reform proposals are not yet possible, we propose more careful study of analogous situations—such as in our postsecondary education system and with international comparisons—to develop the research area and to provide initial evidence.

REFERENCES

Adler, J. Mortimer. 1983. *Paideia Problems and Possibilities*. New York: Macmillan.

Alexander, Karl L. and Martha A. Cook. 1982. "Curricula and coursework: a surprising ending to a familiar story." *American Sociological Review* 47:626–640.

Alexander, Karl L., Gary Natriello, and Aaron M. Pallas. 1985. "For whom the school bell tolls: the impact of dropping out on cognitive performance." *American Sociological Review* 50:409–420.

Allison, Paul D. 1978. "Measures of inequality." *American Sociological Review* 43:865–880.

Astin, Alexander W. 1982. "Excellence and equity in American education." Paper prepared for the National Commission on Excellence in Education.

Austin, Gilbert R. and Herbert Garber, eds. 1982. *The Rise and Fall of National Test Scores*. New York: Academic Press.

Baker, David P. and James M. McPartland. 1982. "Using longitudinal test score data to identify exceptional learning environments." Baltimore: Johns Hopkins University Center for Social Organization of Schools.

Becker, Henry Jay. 1985. "How schools use microcomputers." Baltimore: Johns Hopkins University, Center for Social Organization of Schools.

Block, James H. and Robert B. Burns. 1976. "Mastery learning." Pp. 3–49 in *Review of Research in Education, Vol. 4*, edited by L. S. Shulman. Itasca, IL: Peacock.

Boyer, Ernest L. 1983. *High School*. New York: Harper & Row.

Braddock, Jomills Henry II, Robert L. Crain and James M. McPartland. 1984. "A long-term view of school desegregation: some recent studies of graduates as adults." *Phi Delta Kappan* 66:259–264.

Coleman, James S. 1968. "The concept of equality of educational opportunity." *Harvard Educational Review*, 38:297–310.

Coleman, James S. 1980. "Choice in education." Pp. 233–255 in *The Analysis of Educational Productivity, Vol. 2*, edited by Charles E. Bidwell and D. M. Windham. Cambridge, MA: Ballinger.

Coleman, James S. 1981. "Private schools, public schools, and the public interest." *Public Interest* 64:19–30.

Coleman, James S. 1985. "Inequality in education: evidence on equality and excellence." Paper prepared for the Eighth Goucher College Conference, Baltimore, MD.

Coons, John E. and Steven D. Sugarman. 1977. "Choice and integration: a model statute." Pp. 280–300 in *Parents Teachers, and Children: Prospects for Choice in American Education*, edited by Institute for Contemporary Studies. San Francisco: Institute for Contemporary Studies.

Coons, John E. and Steven D. Sugarman. 1981. *An Initiative for Education by Choice*. San Francisco: Education by Choice.

Crain, Robert L. and Rita E. Mahard. 1983. "The effect of research methodology on desegregation–achievement studies: a meta-analysis." *American Journal of Sociology* 88:839–854.

Cremin, Lawrence A. 1951. *The American Common School: A Historic Conception*. New York: Teachers College Press.

Doyle, Dennis P. and Marsha Levine. 1984. "Magnet schools: choice and quality in public education." *Phi Delta Kappan* 66:265–270.

Edmonds, Ronald R. 1979. "Some schools work and more can." *Social Policy* 9:28–32.

Elam, Stanley M. (ed.). 1978. *A Decade of Gallup Polls of Attitudes Toward Education 1969–1978*. Bloomington, IN: Phi Delta Kappa.

Fenstermacher, Gary D. and John L. Goodlad (eds.). 1983. *Individual Differences and the Common Curriculum*. Chicago: National Society for the Study of Education.

Frank, Charlotte. 1984. "Equity for all students: the New York City promotional gates program." *Educational Leadership*, 41(8):62–65.

Good, Thomas L. and Susan Marshall. 1984. "Do students learn more in heterogeneous or homogeneous groups?" Pp. 15–38 in *The Social Context of Instruction*, edited by Penelope L. Peterson, Louise Cherry Wilkinson, and Maureen T. Hallinan. New York: Academic Press.

Goodlad, John L. 1983. *A Place Called School*. New York: McGraw-Hill.

Greeley, Andrew M. 1977. "Freedom of choice: our commitment to integration." Pp. 183–205 in *Parents, Teachers, and Children: Prospects for Choice in American Education*, edited by Institute for Contemporary Studies. San Francisco: Institute for Contemporary Studies.

Greeley, Andrew M. 1982. *Catholic High Schools and Minority Students*. New Brunswick, NJ: Transaction Books.

Hauser, Robert M., William H. Sewell and Duane F. Alwin. 1976. "High school effects on achievement." Pp. 309–341 in *Schooling and Achievement in American Society*, edited by William H. Sewell, Robert M. Hauser and David L. Featherman. New York: Academic Press.

Heyns, Barbara. 1978. *Summer Learning and the Effects of Schooling*. New York: Academic Press.

Holmes, C. Thomas and Kenneth M. Matthews. 1984. "The effects of non-promotion on elementary and junior high school pupils: a meta-analysis." *Review of Educational Research* 54:225–236.

Howe, Harold II. 1984. "Giving equity a chance in the excellence game." The 1984 Martin Buskin Memorial Lecture. Washington, D.C.: Education Writers Association.

Husen, Torsten. 1979. *The School in Question: A Comparative Study of the School and Its Future in Western Society*. New York: Oxford University Press.

Jackson, Gregg B. 1975. "The research evidence on the effect of grade retention." *Review of Educational Research* 45:613–635.

Jaeger, Richard M. 1982. "The final hurdle: minimum competency achievement testing." Pp. 223–246 in *The Rise and Fall of National Test Scores*, edited by Gilbert R. Austin and Herbert Garber. New York: Academic Press.

James, Estelle and Gail Benjamin. 1984. *Public Versus Private Education: The Japanese Experiment*. New Haven: Yale University Institute for Social and Policy Studies.

Johnson, James R. 1984. "Synthesis of research on grade retention and social promotion." *Educational Leadership* 41(8):66–68.

Klitgaard, Robert E. 1973. *Achievement Scores and Educational Objectives*. Santa Monica, CA: RAND.

Max Planck Institute for Human Development and Education. 1983. *Between Elite and Mass Education: Education in the Federal Republic of Germany*. Albany: State University of New York Press.

McDill, Edward L., Gary Natriello, and Aaron M. Pallas. 1986. "A population at risk: consequences of tougher school standards for student dropouts." *American Journal of Education* 94:135–181.

McPartland, James M. and Edward L. McDill. 1982. "Control and differentiation in the structure of American education." *Sociology of Education* 55:77–88.

Moody, Joseph Nason. 1978. *French Education Since Napoleon*. Syracuse, NY: Syracuse University Press.

Nasaw, David. 1979. *Schooled to Order: A Social History of Public Schooling in the United States*. New York: Oxford University Press.

National Commission on Excellence in Education. 1983. *A Nation at Risk: The Imperative for Educational Reform*. Washington, D.C.: U.S. Government Printing Office.

Okun, Arthur M. 1975. *Equality and Efficiency: The Big Tradeoff*. Washington, D.C.: Brookings Institution.

Peterson, Wilkinson, and Maureen T. Hallinan. 1984. *The Social Context of Instruction*. New York: Academic Press.

Popham, W. James, Keith L. Cruse, Stuart C. Rankin, Paul D. Sandifer, and Paul L. Williams. 1985. "Measurement-driven instruction: it's on the road." *Phi Delta Kappan* 66:628–634.

Resnick, Daniel P. and Lauren B. Resnick. 1985. "Standards, curriculum, and performance: a historical and comparative perspective." *Educational Researcher* 14(4):5–20.

Rhine, W. Ray (ed.). 1981. *Making Schools More Effective: New Directions from Follow Through*. New York: Academic.

Rossell, Christine H. 1985. "Estimating the net benefits of school desegregation reassignments." *Educational Evaluation and Policy Analysis* 7:187–196.

Salganik, Laura Hersh. 1981. "The fall and rise of education vouchers." *Teachers College Record* 83:263–283.

Schwartz, David. 1984. "Update: on minimum competency testing." *Newsnotes: Center for Law and Education* 35:2–3.

Schwartz, John and Christopher Winship. 1980. "The welfare approach to measuring inequality." Pp. 1–36 in *Sociological Methodology*, edited by Karl Schuessler. San Francisco: Jossey-Bass.

Sheppard, Lorrie A. 1983. "Standards for placement and certification." Pp. 61–90 in *On Educational Testing*, edited by Scarvia B. Anderson and John S. Helmick. San Francisco: Jossey-Bass.

Silver, Harold (ed.). 1973. *Equal Opportunity in Education: A Reader in Social Class and Educational Opportunity*. London: Methuen.

Sizer, Theodore R. 1984. *Horace's Compromise: The Dilemma of the American High School*. Boston: Houghton Mifflin.

Slavin, Robert E. 1986. "Ability grouping and student achievement in elementary schools: a best-evidence synthesis." Baltimore: Johns Hopkins University Center for Social Organization of Schools.

Strike, Kenneth A. 1985. "Is there a conflict between equity and excellence?" *Educational Evaluation and Policy Analysis* 7:409–416.

Toch, Thomas. 1984. "The dark side of the excellence movement." *Phi Delta Kappan* 66:173–176.

CHAPTER 7

Implications of an Institutional View of Education for the Study of Educational Effects

JOHN W. MEYER

One can see modern education as a nationwide or worldwide system of organized interaction, structuring the experience and learning of students around the world in regularized ways. The image is that of a standardized processing system. The students being processed, in such a line of thought, are more complex than those of material processing systems but still can be treated as objects of analysis. They vary more in their tractability and in their susceptibility to the treatments of the system. More complex, they vary in their motivation to participate as objects of education. Further, they have their own laws of endogenous development, and therefore appropriate treatment may vary over time. Finally, they vary in various matters of culture or

John W. Meyer • Department of Sociology, Stanford University, Stanford, CA 94305.

perception and in this may relate reflexively to the system that processes them—they may react, for instance, to such expectations as the thought that the degree they get may have value.

Such a view is easy for analysts of education to take in part because the educational system is designed along the lines of such a scientific analysis. Modern education is not primarily the product of the experience of people in families, work situations, political organizations, or armies which slowly accumulated over time to make up a general system. Modern education from its inception arose from general scientific thinking, with backing from ideological elites concerned with the laws of life and growth more than specific training demands. Educational systems are built up around scientific theories of socialization, with rules of sequencing, of curricular structure and interdependence, and of pedagogical method.

Further, these arrays of the laws of the science of education are very highly institutionalized. That is, they are written into very general rules. This has several aspects: First, educational systems are made up of rules providing sweeping standardization across social and physical space. A given grade or curricular step is, by rule, made to mean the same thing across an entire state or society and sometimes takes on a good deal of standard meaning throughout the world. Much of this is highly organized, as when the American nation-state treats, for employment purposes, all high-school graduates alike. Second, in various ways the rules of the science of education are institutionally made true by definition. The sequenced steps of developmental theory are made requirements, as when a high-school diploma is required for university entry. Curricular elements are required components of graduation and graduation of job entry.

The institutionalization of the science of education in a worldwide system of rules gives certain advantages to researchers who want to study school effects. It also creates certain problems.

By way of advantages, the researcher does not require much distinct theory or method, since the science of education structures both. Education is designed to generate individual and collective progress and equality and to resist entropy and inequality. Its success on these axes becomes a main focus of the social sciences of education. The dependent variables are generated by the logic of education itself. So are such independent variables as the forms and stages of treatment and the tests and other evaluations of these that are built into the educational system itself. Hence the central questions of the social science of education: how much does education enhance the achievement and attainment of individuals and society; does it generate equality (eliminating status differences) or reinforce inequalities; and which of various forms of educational treatment work best toward these ends? Method, too, is made easier, and the field is one of the best developed in the social sciences in part for this reason: the educational system collects much of the relevant data and assembles the students in rationalized group structures much more amenable to research access (and on the same terms of comparability the researcher is likely to want—for example with all the sixth-graders together in a room) than any other structure would permit. Note how much easier it is for the IEA, for instance, to assemble data from all over the world on the science achievement of *students* in particular grades than it would be to get reasonable data on what *children* of a particular age are doing in families or peer groups.

But consider also some disadvantages of research when theory and method collapse so completely into the social reality being investigated, no matter how scientized this reality. Findings may reflect the operation of some lawful scientific process natural to the system under investigation. Or they might reflect the fact that the scientific process—as part of the science of education—has been institutionalized and wholly or in part made to be true by various social forces. This is strikingly the case, for instance, with a class of findings most common in the social science research literature on educational effects: a researcher correlates educational attainment with later occupational success, holding some other variables constant, and finds a close relation, concluding that educational attainment produced the occupational success. A common enough, and lawful enough, finding it is. But whose law is involved: the law of the science of education, arguing that education generates virtues which generate success; or the institutionalization of this law in the organizational rules of modern society which build educational requirements into practically every really modern organization in the world? The early social scientists helped create these rules with arguments for meritocracy: their successors (as with the human capital economists) come along and empirically discover the truth the predecessors have laboriously created. Research along such lines can justify the greatest absurdities: It is undoubtedly true that those who know the Latin, as opposed to common, names of bones and other parts of the body are more likely to succeed in medicine—the legal certification of the right to practice medicine may require knowing these names.

The research problem is to distinguish between the effects of schooling and the effects of the instutionalization of schooling, which infuses the system with a kind of "Hawthorne effect." The social authority built into education adds to the incentives to learn and participate. It changes the logic of teaching and organizing instruction. And it alters the rational familial strategies for producing and preparing children for successful life careers. In order to think properly about the effects and organization of schools, this dimension must be taken into account.

In this chapter, rather than considering the institutionalization of education as a peripheral aspect of schooling that may alter schooling effects, we shift further away from the perspective of the science of education itself to emphasize the institutionalization of this science as the central component of modern education. This amounts to seeing educational processing rationality, or socialization theory, not as a set of hypotheses to be investigated but as a cultural or ideological system in its own right with effects of its own. When the rationalities of socialization theory become institutionalized as the secular religion of modern society, they must be analyzed as a religious system.

In the argument below, we spell out hypotheses and research designs along these lines. How does the institutionalization of education affect what young people learn, what they study, what their commitments are, what their capacities are? How does it affect strategies of teachers and school organizers and managers? How does it affect the construction and evolution of the whole educational system?

To begin, we consider a simple example. There is a well institutionalized rule that before young people can obtain the satisfaction and rewards of the highest healing profession, which is the most highly esteemed occupation in our society, they must prove some knowledge of physics and organic chemistry. These young people who wish to become physicians do well to learn, not the arts of healing, but these subjects. Naturally, this learning is higher than it would otherwise be, and so is participation in the relevant institution. And so is commitment. So, we argue, is the relevant academic ability: in preparing for success, young people and their parents are sensitized to the type of thought useful not in healing but in the study of physics and chemistry. (This is especially true given that similar abilities are required for entry into almost all valued professions.)

Further, given such an institutionalized selection system, teachers and administrators would be well advised to focus, not on instruction in healing, but on physics and chemistry. This will produce a better market, more student learning and commitment, and more success.

Now carry the logic one step further. Suppose planners in a disease-ridden and impoverished country wish to improve their medical system. Should they concentrate on the preparation of healers or follow institutionalized lines? The latter will have many advantages—it will receive more internal and external support as legitimate and valuable, elites will be better satisfied, students will see world-conferred value in their work, and so on. Thus, it happens empirically that substantive instruction in physics and organic chemistry can be found in the most unlikely countries in the modern world. And one can take the example many steps further: what is the proper way to teach the necessary physics? Obviously, professional specialists are needed, and university departments, and complete ranges of the appropriate specialties. It follows that one can find education in the full range of modern physics, from quarks to cosmology, all over the world. In many countries this is better developed by far than instruction in the native flora and fauna—or in the native diseases. When the rationality of modern education becomes institutionalized in a religious way, it becomes quite rational to be religious about it.

STATUS AND SUCCESS

It is well known that education is a crucial means to success in all contemporary societies and that educational status works to this end even with measured socialization outcomes held constant. It is all much discussed and often decried as credentialism; in the contemporary literature, it is understood to be institutionalized, a property of the system, not particular schooling organizations: (1) Educational credentials are general requirements (often legally grounded) for social positions. (2) The accreditation of schools' credentials is an aspect of their link to the institutional environment, not an internal structured element.

There appears to be some research reluctance to investigate the value of credentials (independent of the socialization they only loosely index), though the matter is central. Researchers, perhaps because they prefer to subscribe to the science of education rather than to analyze its impact, often invent unmeasured socialization outcomes (e.g., human capital, cultural capital) at the individual level. But it is quite possible to assess the value of educational credentials independent of such matters. Many techniques can be used, among them classic experimental ones in which raters assess the value of individuals varying in described education in various dimensions (e.g., creditworthiness, attractiveness, employability, income, marriageability, electability). One could in such a fashion get a rough range of the institutionalized uses or values of education. Conversely, one would work backward, getting a map of the roles in modern society for which people see education as a necessary or useful credential.

Currently, progress is being made in this area with research comparing institutional settings to see where education matters most in the acquisition credentials. If one assumes that credential value, rather than substantive socialized qualities produced by education, is at issue, a good deal can be learned. In occupational allocation, for instance, educational credentials are especially valued by larger organizations (Stolzenberg, 1978) linked to public status (Collins, 1979), especially the nation-state (Meyer *et al.*, 1979). Research in the area, however, remains primitive, in part because of a continuing inclination to look for some individual-level rationality behind the credential-granting rules, or that individual property which it is assumed education must signal (Spence, 1973; Thurow, 1975).

LEARNING

We can turn now to the most obvious educational outcome, cognitive learning. The greater the institutionalization of education, the more students learn (Meyer, 1980). This should be true with such other factors as the amount and kind of institution held constant.

One can distinguish component ideas here. The greater the value of education and the more thorough its monopoly over success, the more complete the immersion in the student role. And the more complete the social identification of a topic with the definition of education, the more students should learn.

These would be easy matters for research were researchers inclined to step back from the science of education to an analysis of the institutionalization of this science. And much research of the experimental kind traditional in the field would be feasible. Do students learn more if they are in the student role?

Getting credit? Taught by people identified as teachers? Learning material clearly identified as belonging to categories of schooled knowledge (e.g., mathematics)? It is easy enough to manipulate the institutional meaning of standard institutional stimuli experimentally, looking for effects on learning. The point would be to vary the states of the stimuli and also the state of the learner (from student to young person).

Ideas of this general kind have strong macrosociological implications, though some of these are hard to examine empirically with related factors (e.g., rates of student participation or instructional time) held constant. The worldwide shift to the use of education as a general requirement for success has probably increased how much students learn. Further, the expansion of the standard subject matter of education has undoubtedly increased the range of subjects young people learn and remember. At the same time, some subjects (spelling, perhaps geography, numerical operations) may have moved away from a status as core to educated knowledge.

Research on learning, comparing societies and sectors and making comparisons over historical time, is most relevant here. Findings are always subject to multiple interpretations—differential learning may reflect variation in curricular emphasis or student participation rather than learning with participation held constant, but they can be suggestive nevertheless. Recent examples of such discussions include those of the IEA international comparisons, (e.g., Heyneman and Loxley, 1983), the American test score decline, or international studies deriving from the work of Piaget.

The general point here is that the institutionalization of education binds the young person to the student role, ties more and more educational content to this role, and adds value to the whole nexus as a general desideratum and as a means to other ends. It thus increases learning. The same techniques of education would be less effective if they were not so authoritative. Put another way, its social authority may be the most central technique of education.

Note that these effects, like many we discuss, follow from the institutionalization of education, not characteristics of particular schools or classrooms. Institutionalization varies across societies, time, sectors, and topics of the curriculum. Studies that restrict themselves to variation among organizations within a common context would not show the effects involved.

PARTICIPATION AND ATTENTION

The arguments above suppose that institutionalization affects learning with such other factors as participation held constant. But we should expect very large effects on participation as well, both through efforts of students and those of the system, which we discuss below.

At the student level, we may expect participation rates in education to increase as (a) education becomes the mediation for more kinds of success and (b) education acquires a monopoly over status conferral. Thus, the long-run expansion in years of schooling, days of schooling per year, and attendance rates are partly driven by the ever-increasing importance of education as the crucial mechanism for social attainment. The question can be studied by comparing communities and status groups (Stinchcombe, 1964), rural and urban sectors, societies, and time. More refined studies can tease out the effects on participation as curricular elements become more or less important across time or organizational setting. Detailed analyses can show which groups, holding constant personal interests, participate in and attend which subjects the most. Common observation, for instance, suggests massive overenrollment in mathematics (compared with the distribution of student interest) because it is central to later attainment.

One can also study such questions experimentally, varying the centrality of a topic and watching student participation rates change. We suppose that, *ceteris paribus*, students are more likely to show up for a class that is (a) required, (b) for credit,

(c) prerequisite for later preferred curricula and occupations, (d) given a central label like mathematics, (e) taught by a regularly certified teacher.

Overall, there have been extraordinary expansions of educational participation in every country, such that perhaps 19 or 20 percent of the world's population are now students (UNESCO, 1955–83). This has happened over recent decades with little popular resistance. Obviously, the linking of education, through careful sequencing rules, with the central values and opportunities of societal cultures and stratification systems is involved.

COMMITMENT AND CAPACITY

Behind learning, in a causal chain, lie participation on the one side and capacity on the other. Students with the appropriate mentality—intelligence—learn more in schooling. And clearly, participation in more schooling, at the individual level, increases intellectual capacity. We are concerned, however, with the effects of the institutionalization of education. The general point can be put simply: apart from their individual experience with education, the intelligence of a population is increased as education becomes a more central mediator of success and value. As people learn that education is crucial, they learn to think in ways appropriate to schooling. They acquire the appropriate rationalism, orientation to individual action and calculation, and so on. There is much evidence of contextual or societal effects here (Cole and Means, 1981; Cole and Scribner, 1981; Inkeles and Smith, 1974; Stevenson, 1978), independent of the educational experience of children or their parents. The evidence is less well developed than it should be because, given the research inclination to think of intelligence as partly genetic, finding societal differences seems to come embarrassingly close to racism. But it is quite obvious that societies differ in the extent to which they generate individuated "intelligence" and that this variable is closely related to the institutionalization of education.

It seems likely that the relation is causal and that the institutionalization of education, more than other modern structures, directly produces a cultural emphasis on individuated intelligence. Precisely because this variable is at the individual level so determinative of education much more than other success, societies that make educational success crucial put great premiums on intelligence. Individuals and families react to this. Modern forms of child rearing, as opposed to child management, result, with the construction of the active, individuated, intelligent child. Societal variation on this dimension is probably one source of the great national variation in learning the IEA studies discover. Further, the cultural emphasis on intelligence resulting from the institutionalization of education generates not only higher aggregate differentials but also more variance and greater correlation with social resources. Heyneman and Loxley (1983), in a reanalysis of IEA data, show that correlations between social status and school learning (known to be heavily affected by intelligence) greatly increase in more highly developed societies. This result would follow from the institutionalization of education, which creates more incentives for families with more resources to devote them to modern forms of child rearing. The same result also appears in studies of summer learning (Heyns, 1978). If education and its value are sufficiently institutionalized, children will continue to focus on it during vacation at least in the higher strata.

Thus, the institutionalization of education, over and above education itself, raises the schooling competence of a population and makes this competence a dimension of social stratification. Much more comparative research is needed here.

The discussion above, for simplicity, assumes intelligence to be a single and constant dimension. This is unlikely, and we can suggest variations in the way in which individuated intelligence might be organized depending on the institutionalization of education in a society. For instance, the broader the topics or domain of education and its curricula in a society, the wider ought to be the range of indicators linked to the concept. In a society like our own with a very wide range of schooled

topics there should be a very broad domain of intellectualiza-
tion, including such matters as emotional expression.

LIFELONG LEARNING

The example above suggests that the institutionalization
of education affects parts of the individual life cycle before
education begins. Children anticipate, and parents go to great
lengths to help them anticipate education. They try to become
intelligent, to learn the relevant skills and values, and to acquire
the appropriate orientations. Childhood, as Ariès (1962) and
Illich (1971) suggest, becomes more schooled.

But not only childhood. After the schooling period itself,
education is a requirement built into occupation and social status. Actors who have acquired positions based on education or
who function in a society with the value of education institutionalized can be expected continually to reinterpret their experiences and competence in education terms. Holding constant
their own educations, people in more schooled societies should
show such effects—measured by inclination to summarize occupational or personal skills in schooled language, to construct
the appropriate documents, and to build schoollike training
programs even in the posteducational stages of life. One expects
to find, in such societies, schooled instruction in everything
from sex or childbearing to the dangers of nuclear war.

The research issue here is to show the impact of the institutionalization of education on the learning and involvement
of those outside the system. We imagine that the more central
an institution education is, the more education-related com-
petences are maintained or acquired both before and after the
educational period itself. Further, we argue that correlation of
social status and education-related competencies would be
enhanced by the institutionalization of education.

Comparative research would be useful here. We are arguing that all sorts of schoollike knowledge—say, the manner of

government and location of countries and capitals—will in schooled societies (with individual education held constant) be more closely related to social status and less closely related to such properties as life-cycle status or experience.

THE ORGANIZATION OF TEACHING AND SCHOOLING

The power of education, we have argued above, lies in the *institutional* rules that give it widespread meaning and binding authority over the future of students. The implied contrast here is with education as a system of organized interaction, interpersonal meaning, and immediately relevant content. Students show up in school and attend to content not because it is interesting and relevant to their experience, but because it is *education* and by institutional rule relevant to their future. They choose instruction because of educational relevance, not out of liking or friendship for teachers.

Given this situation, teachers and schools make efforts to align themselves with the institutional rules of education, from which their power and capacity are derived, rather than attending to their effectiveness as systems of interaction. Many features of schools and classrooms follow from this fundamental situation, which means that schools and teachers try to be more educationally conservative—and gain both support and effectiveness by this strategy—than might otherwise be the case (Meyer and Rowan, 1978): As a first instance, both teachers and schools package instruction in traditional categories rather than attempting to establish much relevance. They gain the general authority built into the institutional rules defining these categories. What looks like curricular inertia is really active reliance on institutional authority.

Further, teachers and schools emphasize much more traditional pedagogical technique than would make sense for a technology of *interpersonal* instruction. The whole-class lecture method survives more and succeeds better than prevailing theory explains. This method, by concealing variability in attention, activity, and understanding, dramatizes the widely institutionalized fact of standardized content. Teacher and standardized student become immersed in the ritual authority of the system.

Finally, variability among schools, teachers, and pupils is concealed, reinforcing ritual standardization: First, teaching work is little inspected, thus reinforcing the norm of its standard character. Second, the enormous variability in actual curricular content is concealed in a limited number of standard fields and courses of study. And third, great variability in student learning is concealed, as aggregate data are hidden, tests are designed to be idiosyncratic and noncomparable, and individual student variability is kept private in grades. The triumph of the system, from the whole-class method to the system of standard curricular categories, is that even in a situation in which no student really knows what is going on, the pressures to keep going are maintained by the maintenance of the appearance of education.

Our point is that in a system in which institutional rules are a driving force, *appearances matter*, and maintaining them may be a central means to effectiveness. This of course makes the decoupling of actual instruction and learning from these appearances advantageous. The institutional system gains power and effectiveness if variations in effects are concealed.

Of course, this standardization of appearance produced by teachers and schools, and their submission to the larger authority of the whole institution, means that in general effects of practical organizational variations among institutionally similar settings will be very small. The literature is filled with searches for the true reality of education beneath the appearances—the true source of contextual variations. But the appearances *are* in the main the important reality and all the parties involved, including students, can see this reality behind the idiosyncratic technique of particular teachers or structures of particular schools. The literature has not really confronted this relative success of bad teachers and schools as an explanatory problem.

EDUCATIONAL CHANGE

It is conventional for critics of education, observing its decoupled character, to see it as unchanging. It is indeed true that efforts at planned organizational change are sabotaged by the institutionalized aspects of education. Yet one finds much change in education, with sweeping national movements reconstructing it one way or another.

The resolution to this inconsistency is to attend to the institutionalized character of the system but not to see the institutions involved as unchanging. Educational organization is relatively impenetrable because it is a relatively decoupled set of structures linked closely to institutional rules: that means that change occurs more through institutional than organizational mechanisms. The broad liberalization of the late 1960s occurred more through public and professional understandings than through specific organizational decisions—and one can find indications of the liberalism both where rules were changed and where they were not. Similarly, the tightening up of the past recessionary decade has been nationwide, with its symbols appearing in all sorts of schools and classrooms. Again one finds evidence of this both in schools, districts, or states where the organization rules have changed and where they have not.

A broader look would now show that educational trends— precisely because the system is so highly institutionalized—are often worldwide, as with secondary-school reform of the 1960s and 1970s and current worldwide discoveries of inefficiency, lack of learning, and weakness of discipline. Such themes shift about on a worldwide basis and can create rather rapid changes in local educational agendas. Particular decision makers may have little impact, exactly because so many aspects of the system are controlled by institutional rather than organizational rules.

SOCIETAL EFFECTS

Once one sees the educational system as a network of highly institutionalized rules rather than as student individuals being processed, broader classes of effects which do not occur through these individual students become plausible (Meyer, 1977). Educational rules which define bodies of knowledge as extent, and classes of personnel as controlling and possessing this knowledge, can obviously have a large impact on society.

In contemporary thinking, one general effect of this sort may be especially noted. Educational institutions provide a certain social location for all sorts of knowledge which may or may not exist in some experiential sense. They thus make possible the expansion of modern social organization into sectors previously considered invisible, or highly uncertain. Consider, for instance, the affect of the educational certification, and professional establishment, of sex therapists. Expansions of medical practice, the insurance system, and all sorts of research ventures become possible immediately.

The general effect, of which this example is an illustration, is the overall expansion of the service sector in modern society. This sector, more than agriculture or industry, has been the most rapidly expanding social sector even in the poorer countries of the world in recent decades (Fiala, 1984). This rapid expansion strikingly coincides with the expansion of educational systems, and we are arguing for a causal relation. The institutionalization of so many forms of educational competence as authoritative leads to the organizational expansion of all sorts of activities that once would have seemed unstable, illegitimate, invisible, and uncertain.

These types of effects of education occur at the societal level, not necessarily mediated by the production of particular eduated people of one sort or another. They are effects that arise as the institutional rules of education (e.g., certificational authority) buttress particular organizational changes in society through legal changes, ideological changes, cultural changes, and so on. The elaboration of educational rationalities makes possible alterations in other rationalized institutions (Meyer and Rowan, 1978).

CONCLUSIONS

We have called attention to the consequences of the extraordinary institutionalization in widespread and binding rule systems of education in modern society. The institutionalization, over and above education itself, adds greatly to the effects of education on individuals. And it changes the nature of reasonable strategies for educators, too, who gain power through immersion in widespread rules as ritual rather than through locally effective action and decisions. And one can see direct effects on society as well.

In all these matters, though, the methodological nature of research in this field needs some modification. The arguments we make above suggest effects of education that might not be distinctive to particular schools and classrooms but are characteristic of whole contexts in which particular educational rules are institutionalized. Institutionally defined types of schools matter more than particular schools; types of classrooms more than individual classrooms; and variation among the national societies within which the rules of education are often homogeneous become central. Our arguments call for comparative research among contexts more than among schools and classrooms. We have suggested how this might be done with comparative research and in a number of instances with experimental studies that vary contextual assumptions.

There is a curious reluctance, in this field, to suspend faith in the science of education for purposes of analysis. The science of education proposes to examine variations in the effects of instructional techniques and social relationships in schools and classrooms. Researchers, despite little success, continue on with the same effort. They resist looking at variations in *institutional* context—between countries, for example, or between tracks endowed with sharply different rights, or between students and nonstudents—as if the effects of these were trivial or obvious. But it is exactly the feature of modern education that it has the power of the obviously authoritative. The power of its certification is so penetrating for just this reason: our argument is that we should investigate the effects of variations in this power and thus consider variations in institutional context.

REFERENCES

Ariès, Philippe. 1962. *Centuries of Childhood*. New York: Vintage.

Cole, Michael and Barbara Means. 1981. *Comparative Studies of How People Think*. Cambridge: Harvard University Press.

Cole, Michael and Sylvia Scribner. 1981. *The Psychology of Literacy*. Cambridge: Harvard University Press.

Collins, Randall. 1979. *The Credential Society: A Historical Sociology of Education and Stratification*. New York: Academic Press.

Fiala, Robert Alan. 1984. The International System and the Dynamics of Service Sector Growth in Lesser Developed Countries, 1950–80. Unpublished doctoral dissertation, Stanford University.

Heyneman, Stephen and William Loxley. 1983. "The effect of primary-school quality on academic achievement across twenty-nine high- and low-income countries." *American Journal of Sociology* 88:1162–94.

Heyns, Barbara. 1978. *Summer Learning and the Effects of Schooling*. New York: Academic Press.

Illich, Ivan. 1971. *Deschooling Society*. New York: Harper & Row.

Inkeles, Alex and David H. Smith. 1974. *Becoming Modern: Individual Change in Six Developing Countries*. Cambridge: Harvard.

Meyer, John W. 1977. "The effects of education as an institution." *American Journal of Sociology* 83:55–77.

Meyer, John W. 1980. "Levels of the educational system and schooling effects. Pp. 15–63 in Charles E. Bidwell and Douglas M. Windham (eds.), *The Analysis of Educational Productivity, Vol. 2*. Cambridge: Ballinger.

Meyer, John and Brian Rowan. 1978. "The structure of educational organizations." In Marshall Meyer (ed.), *Environments and Organizations*. San Francisco: Jossey-Bass.

Meyer, John W., David Tyack, Joane P. Nagel, and Audri Gordon. 1979. "Public education as nationbuilding in America." *American Journal of Sociology* 85:591–613.

Spence, Michael. 1973. "Job market signalling." *Quarterly Journal of Economics* 87:355–75.

Stevenson, Harold William. 1978. *Schooling, Environment, and Cognitive Development*. Chicago: University of Chicago Press.

Stinchcombe, Arthur L. 1964. *Rebellion in a High School*. Chicago: Quadrangle Books.

Stolzenberg, Ross M. 1978. "Bringing the boss back in." *American Sociological Review* 43:813–828.

Thurow, Lester. 1975. *Generating Inequality*. New York: Basic Books.

UNESCO. 1955–83. *Statistical Yearbook*. Louvain: UNESCO.

CHAPTER 8

The Relations between School and Social Structure

JAMES S. COLEMAN

Two quite different orientations toward schooling can be found throughout its history. These two orientations have created a dilemma for educational policy that has never been satisfactorily resolved. First, schools have been seen as the society's instrument to release a child from the blinders imposed by accident of birth into this family or that family. They have been designed to open broad horizons to the child, transcending the limitations of the parents. They have taken children from disparate cultural backwaters into the mainstream of a nation's culture. They have been a major element in social mobility, freeing children from the poverty of their parents and the low status of their social origins. They have been a means of stripping away identities of ethnicity and social origin and implanting a common identity.

A second orientation to schooling sees school as an extension of the family. It is an aid to the family, by reinforcing its values. The school is *in loco parentis*, vested with the authority

James S. Coleman • Department of Sociology, University of Chicago, Chicago, IL 60637.

of the parent to carry out the parent's will. The school is, in this orientation, an efficient means for transmitting the culture of the community from the older generation to the younger. It is an extension of the parent's will, which helps create the next generation in the image of the preceding one.

These two orientations are not in fundamental conflict. When the community is an extension of the family, when the society is a homogeneous nation that is an extension of the communities within it, and when the state expresses the aims of the homogeneous nation, then these two orientations coincide for most families. But when one or more of these conditions does not hold, a conflict arises. Some illustrations follow:

• In the young nineteenth-century United States, a homogeneous Protestant English-origin population had established schools that expressed its cultural, religious, and philosophical values and served simultaneously the family's, community's, and nation's interests. For a new set of immigrants, Irish and Catholic, these two orientations came into direct conflict: the religious values and customs transmitted to these schools directly conflicted with those of the family, the culture transmitted was the culture of the English-origin natives, and the result was an alienating environment for their children. In turn, the Irish Catholic schools they established, outside the public school system, were seen as a threat by those in the community and the society transmitting the dominant Protestant English culture.

• The massive German immigration to the United States resulted in many rural communities in parts of the Midwest (Ohio, Illinois, Kansas, Nebraska, Wisconsin, and other states) that were culturally and linguistically German. In these communities, the cultural, linguistic, and religious conflicts were resolved in various ways. In some cases, children of the immigrants were taken into the public schools and imbued with a language, culture, and ideals foreign to those of their immigrant parents. In some cases, Lutheran or Catholic schools were established outside the public school system, the school constituting for the family an alternative community that would transmit at least the religious values of the parents and would keep the children from being wholly absorbed by the main-stream culture. In some cases, the cleavage came between the community and the society, resulting in public schools reflecting the family's and community's German background: Instruction was in German, and the school transmitted a culture which at many points was alien to the dominant culture. Some of these public schools retained the German language until transformed by the nationalistic fervor that accompanied World War I.

• In the Federal Republic of Germany, the "guestworkers" that have accompanied economic growth since the 1960s brought a new set of children into ethnically and culturally homogeneous schools: Turkish, Yugoslav, Spanish, and others. For some, such as Turks, even religious holidays were different. Here, the matter has been even further compounded by the fact that most of these children are not German citizens and the permanancy of their immigration is uncertain for many. They are being socialized by the schools into a culture that is only tentatively central to their future.

• In the southern United States, the cultural conflict between the white-dominant segregationist orientation of the families, communities, and even the region, and the egalitarian, colorblind orientation dominant in the nation as a whole came to a head with the Brown decision of 1954. Through a long and painful process extending into the 1970s, the schools underwent a transformation from expressions of the local segregationist orientation to expressions of the colorblind orientation characteristic of the nation. Some white families created segregationist academies in the private sector, schools that were extensions of their own cultural values.

• The late 1960s was a period of high value conflict in the United States, between the dominant traditional values of the generation in control and values extolling freedom for youth and release from the narrow views of the past. Some parents and teachers established "free schools" and "alternative schools" outside the public system, in which children were participants in creating their curriculum and in which the traditional classroom was abandoned in favor of more active, participative modes of learning. Some schools and some schools-within-schools in the public sector also took on the form of alternative schools.

• In the 1970s and 1980s, a number of conservative Christian schools and evangelical Christian schools have been established in the United States by parents concerned about the values transmitted by the public schools, secular and in opposition to Christian virtues as they perceive them. These schools represent attempts to recreate a cultural and value homogeneity for the children that insulates them from the values permeating the larger society.

These examples of conflict between the family as the primary agent of socialization and the schools as means of emancipation from the family show the diverse settings in which the conflict arises, as well as its fundamental character. As the examples indicate, it is not a conflict in which parents are always right nor one in which the forces of emancipation from parents are always right, from the point of view of the child. But the necessity to add this last phrase, "from the point of view of the child," should give us pause. The phrase suggests that schools are designed to carry out certain goals for the benefit of children as individuals and that it is these goals in terms of which they must be evaluated. Indeed, that is the common view of schools, and most evaluations of their functioning take these individualistic goals as the criteria, assuming that the interests of children can be taken as given.

But the necessity for adding the phrase indicates that the matter is not so simple. The struggles over control of the school, as exemplified in the cases described above, show that schools are not merely for children, regarded as individuals whose interests and goals can be assumed. Schools are for families, for communities, for cultural groups, for societies, for religious groups, for local governments, and for central governments. Recognition of this fact is important, for it implies that school policy is *not* solely aimed toward goals for children as individuals, however insistent the rhetoric surrounding policy. It implies also that evaluation of the functioning of schools cannot be limited to the individualistic goals they achieve for children, goals upon which consensus is assumed. They must be evaluated as well according to goals that these different groups hold for them. And these are goals that are often in conflict and on which there will not be consensus.

Recognizing that schools are not merely for children as individuals leads to the asking of broader questions about how schools function from the point of view not of the child but of these various groups whose goals may be in conflict. In order to do that, it is useful to gain a sense of the current setting in which schools operate in the United States.

CULTURAL CLEAVAGES AND SOCIAL LACUNAE IN AMERICA

A setting in which there are not conflicts between the school as extension of the family and the school as emancipator of the child from the family is one in which there is perfect value consistency and social structural continuity between family and society. It is an ideal that occurs only in the absence of social change, and only in small homogeneous societies, perhaps best exemplified by primitive tribes before the penetration of modern civilization, or by homogeneous ethnic groups. Those settings differ in two principal ways from the settings found in current Western society. First, there is social structural consistency. The adults whom children see and know outside the home—both in and out of school—are adults closely linked to the family. The other young people whom children see and know are children of these same adults linked to the family.

Second, and in part stemming from the social consistency, there is value consistency. The values to which children are exposed are the values of these same adults, not far removed socially from the family. There is value consistency between children and their friends, between parents and their friends, and between parents and their children.

Schools, in such a setting of structural consistency and value consistency, reinforce both. They provide a locus and occasion for transmission of the generally held values and also a social context within which children whose parents know each other and hold similar values can interact.

Such a setting is not necessarily idyllic, of course. It is an "ideal type," representing a pure case of a certain form of social organization. But it has no mechanism for change, and it may be dull or oppressive to those embedded within it. Here it serves for us only the usefulness of a comparison and contrast to modern Western society.

The two elements of structural consistency and value consistency, although often found together, are nevertheless analytically distinct and are sometimes empirically separated as well. To give a sense of what is meant by structural consistency, I will give an extended illustration of schools in two communities.

STRUCTURAL CONSISTENCY AND FUNCTIONAL COMMUNITIES

The first community is in the heart of Appalachia. The county is Tucker County, West Virginia, a rural and mountainous county largely covered by forest. It has only one town of any size, Parsons, the county seat, population 1,937. There is one high school for the county, several elementary schools that go up to the fifth grade, and one middle school, with sixth, seventh, and eighth grades. One of the elementary schools is a school with three teachers. The first and second grades are together, the third, fourth, and fifth grades are together, and there is a head teacher—although the grade combinations vary each year, depending on the sizes of the cohorts. The teachers are from the local community. Parents know them well, both directly and through the extended network of kinship, friendship, and work relations that pervade each of the communities served by the school and connect these communities.

Some of the fathers of children in the school work in the mines, some have farms (not productive enough to make a living) which they combine with other jobs like driving a school bus, some are engaged in community services like operating a gas station and general store or delivering mail. In the county seat, the jobs are more diversified, including jobs in the bank or working for the state or the county, or insurance agent or barber. Some of the men are on unemployment compensation, and a few families are on welfare; until the mines reopened a few years ago, many more were. Some are on workmen's compensation, and one, who had children late in life by an Indian woman he found in Mexico, is on workmen's compensation for injuries in the mines. A number of the older generation receive black lung compensation.

Because many of the fathers' work is near home, and because there is work around the house, yard, and garden, fathers are around their children when the children are not in school. They sometimes play with the younger children, but the form of interaction changes somewhere between five and nine. The fathers' activities are physical and often outdoors, and the boys tag along, trying to engage in their fathers' activities. They emulate their fathers, whether riding four-wheelers, a motorcycle, drinking beer, trying to chew tobacco, or hunting raccoons.

Most of the mothers do not work outside the home, but some do, in the local shoe factory or in clerical jobs in the county seat. Many of the grandparents of school children live in the community, as do many of their aunts, uncles, cousins, and other relatives. Few parents have gone beyond high school, and many never completed high school. Most of the children will not go beyond high school, but some will—and most of those who do will leave the county, because of the absence of work in the county other than jobs of the sort described. Thus depleted, the next generation that remains in the county will continue to consist primarily of high-school graduates and dropouts.

There is a weekly newspaper published in the county seat, and most weeks it contains extended news about children in school: competition for queen for the county fair, or the queen's court, which includes grade-school children, or homecoming

queen, or football games, or car accidents involving local teen-
agers who have had too much to drink, or trouble with the law
that some local boys have had.

The second community is similarly unusual, though in
many respects at an opposite extreme from the one I have just
described. It is the community surrounding the University of
Chicago, Hyde Park. Most of the faculty (about 70 percent) of
the University of Chicago live in Hyde Park or Kenwood, within
a mile of the university. Many walk or ride a bicycle to work;
those who come by car drive only a few blocks.

The Hyde Park community has several public elementary
schools and three private schools, two of them religiously affiliated, and one a university laboratory school. There is a single
large public high school, and a private high school, the laboratory school.

The laboratory elementary school is much larger than the
elementary school in Tucker County with three teachers. Here,
there are three or four classes per grade. Many of the teachers
live in the community, though few are closely connected to the
university community. Some parents know their children's
teachers outside school, but most do not. They do know them
secondhand, by reputation through the extended network of
friendship, neighborhood, and work relations that pervade Hyde
Park and Kenwood. Kinship relations are largely missing,
though there are examples of family "dynasties" who were at
or affiliated with the University of Chicago schools through
virtually their whole lives. The most prominent are Edward
and Julian Levi, brothers who began in the laboratory nursery
school and who have recently retired from posts at the university as president and professor of law.

One or both parents of most children in the school work
at the university, either as faculty or staff. Others live in Hyde
Park (or adjacent Kenwood) and are connected only by friendship relations and neighborhood associations to those in the
university community. A few live outside the area and are not
connected to these networks. The youngest children are often
brought to school on foot by fathers or mothers on their way
to work at the university.

More of the lab school mothers than Tucker County mothers are employed outside the home, many at the university. They are less often involved together through church or local homemaker groups than is true in Tucker County but are involved in some neighborhood groups. There are few *family* gatherings at which gossip flows about children, teachers, and school; but there are many *social* gatherings at which such gossip flows.

Nearly all the students at the lab school will go on to college; many will obtain advanced degrees. A few of those will remain in the community, but most will leave. Their families will be succeeded by others, similar in education and life style, but geographically mobile, in contrast to the Tucker County families.

Before drawing any conclusions about these schools and communities, and before making more explicit comparisons, I will describe an incident in each which will facilitate the comparisons.

Event 1 (in the Tucker County school): The first day of school, a fourth-grader reported to her mother that her first-grade sister (who is shy and verbally backward) had cried most of the time, and the head teacher, Mrs. X, had yelled at her, which made her cry even more. The mother called the first-grade teacher and asked her all about it, then called two friends to talk to them about Mrs. X. The fourth-grader reported on the second day that much the same thing had happened with her first-grade sister. The mother talked again to friends about the events. The third day the mother went to the school, confronted Mrs. X, and discussed her first-grade daughter. By the week's end, the daughter seemed to have accepted school and had stopped crying, and Mrs. X had stopped yelling. Nevertheless, at a barbecue on Saturday of that week, most of the gossip among the four women (two of whom had had children in the school, and one who would have the next year) was about the school and the teacher—with occasional remarks from one of the men, who knew and did not like Mrs. X's husband.

Event 2 (in the Hyde Park school): Last spring, a faculty member at the University of Chicago realized that his son, in nursery school, would be put in one of the two kindergarten classes. He talked to a colleague in his department, who said vehemently, "Don't let him be put in Mrs. A's class. She is terrible for boys who don't do just what she expects." His son had had that teacher when the teacher taught second grade and had finally adjusted to school after being moved to another class. When the nursery school father spoke to a second colleague in his department who had had two sons in the school, he heard a similar story about Mrs. A and one of the sons.

The mother talked to some friends and got a more differentiated story about Mrs. A: she was strict and demanding and not good for children (especially boys) whose progress was slow. The two parents talked at length to the nursery school teacher, Mrs. B—a long-time nursery school teacher with experience in following her "graduates" in Mrs. A's and other teachers' classes. They talked as well to other nursery school parents whose children were friends of their son. On the basis of Mrs. B's experience, they decided collectively to try, after all, to have their children put in Mrs. A's class. This fall, this set of friends all began school in Mrs. A's class— with their parents especially attentive because of the warnings they had heard.

These two events are sufficient to introduce the more explicit examination of social consistency. As may be evident by this point, I am suggesting that despite the enormous differences between these two communities, between the futures of the children that are in them, and between the schools that serve these children, there are some strong similarities. I want to suggest that most public schools in the United States are sharply different from these two schools and are becoming more different all the time. The similarities between these two schools, and their contrast with most American schools, lie in the strength of the functional communities they serve. The Tucker County school serves a functional community built around work, kinship, residence, church, and local associations. The Hyde Park school serves a functional community built primarily around work and residence.

Perhaps the most important property of these functional

communities, for our purpose here, can without too much distortion be expressed in a sentence: The friends and associates of a child in school are children of friends and associates of the child's parents (see Figure 1A). In contrast, Figure 1B, representing absence of a functional community spanning generations, does not show this closure.

Going back over the two events that I described, involving the Tucker County first-grader and the Hyde Park kindergartner, it should be evident that closure something like that of Figure A was critical to the actions taken by the parents. Without the closure, in a social structure like that shown in Figure B, the Tucker County mother would not have had the informational reinforcement that encouraged her to go to the school and talk to the head teacher. She would have been reduced to

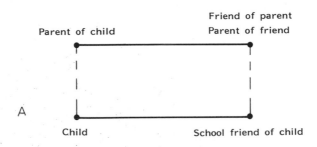

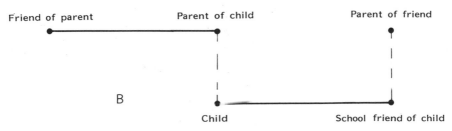

Figure 1. Closure (A) and lack of closure (B) among parents of children in school.

her individual inner resources, and for most parents these are not sufficiently strong to impel actions of the sort this mother took. The intimidation of the school is far too strong.

Schools with intergenerational closure bring certain *benefits*, and they bring certain *costs*. First, the benefits.

THE BENEFITS OF INTERGENERATIONAL CLOSURE

Information flow of the sort exhibited in the events in the Tucker County first grade or the Hyde Park kindergarten is one feedback support provided to the parent by a functional community with closure of the sort shown in Figure A, but it is not the only one. In such a community, the parent need not depend on the child itself for information about its behavior, in school and out. The parent has additional channels through the friends and acquaintances of the child, those children's parents, and back to the parent. The parent has a set of sentinels, each imperfect but taken together capable of providing a rich texture of information about the child's behavior. In the absence of this closure, the last link of the feedback chain is missing, and there are no sentinels. The child's behavior can remain unnoticed and unattended by adults whom the parents know, and the parent is again unsupported—this time in negotiations not with the school but with the child.

It is this feedback structure that is the most important property for parents of a functional community with intergenerational closure. And the greatest value of the feedback structure to parents lies in its aid to their own task of raising their children. A common complaint of modern parents is their defenselessness against pleas from a child, "A's mother lets her do X; it's not fair if I can't," or "All the other guys' parents let them do Y, why can't I?" The absence of parental defense lies in the lack of knowledge about what the daughter's friend *is* allowed to do by her mother, or just what the "other guys' parents" will let them do. Children, knowing the absence of closure among their parents, exploit it, working back and forth to loosen parental rules. In some cases, parents of students in school have in desperation attempted to establish formally a set of principles governing the rights and responsibilities of children in the school and community.

The existence of intergenerational closure creates a very different pattern. Mothers, in the course of gossip and casual conversation, will have occasion to discuss contingencies in their children's behavior and activities before they occur. These discussions lead to establishing norms for their children's activities, norms that they know will be reinforced by parents of their children's friends. Maintenance of the norms is in the interest of all parents, and in a sufficiently close functional community, parents will sanction not only their own children, but their children's friends (i.e., their friends' children) as well. In contrast, when the functional community exists only among children, and parents are in a fragmented social structure, they may not feel free to sanction their own children.

Power, which in the absence of intergenerational closure is in the hands of the children (who maintain a thriving functional community in their own age group, facilitated by the school), is in the hands of parents when such closure exists. They are armed with a set of norms and aid one another in the enforcement of the norms.

There are other consequences of intergenerational closure as well. In a structure with closure, like that of Figure A, relationships easily spring up along the diagonal of the figure: between a child and an adult other than that child's parents. Intergenerational friendships arise. In Tucker County, a man will introduce his neighbor's son, along with his own, to the complexities of trapping, or a grandfather will help his grandson to raise a calf for 4-H.

In Hyde Park, there are fewer friendships across generations, but there are some: A faculty member takes on a colleague's high-school-age child as a research assistant, or a runner whom a faculty member sees at the field house will teach his friend's son about training to be a competitive runner.

In a structure without closure, as in Figure B, the child's

principal relations with adults are—except for teachers—with its own parents. There is little reason for an adult to take an interest in other people's children. Indeed, any such interest is suspect, given the potential for child exploitation, sexual or otherwise. But when the closure exists, in a structure like that of Tucker County or Hyde Park, there are many adults, other than the child's own parents, to take an interest in the child.

The peculiar character of the open structure between adults and children is that it fails to encourage relations between children and adults who are not their parents; when such relations do occur, it cannot monitor them to guard against exploitation of child by adult. There is simultaneously, throughout society, a decline in the number of volunteer youth leaders, such as scoutmasters, or boys and girls club leaders, and an increase in concern about sexual exploitation of children by adults— both a consequence, if my conjectures are correct, of the decline of functional communities with intergenerational closure.

The interest of adults other than parents in a child has important motivating consequences as well. The same information channels that let the parent know about a child's misbehavior and failings also let the community know about the child's successes, in school and out. And the same relations that develop along the diagonal between children and adults bring rewards to the child from these adults when successes occur. The child receives rewards, status, and respect not only from parents—as is true even in the most anomic urban setting— but also from other adults in the community. The parent shares in those rewards as well, and both parent and child are encouraged toward further efforts.

THE COSTS OF INTERGENERATIONAL CLOSURE

Along with the benefits of a functional community with intergenerational closure come costs. The principal cost is the exclusionary and separatist tendencies it can produce. Corresponding to the richness of social texture within the community is a weakness of links to the outside. Some private schools, as well as some within the public sector, may be seen as attempts by functional communities of adults to provide intergenerational closure to their functional community, to create a school in which the friends of their children are the children of their friends. These communities can be described as "intentional communities," borrowing a term used mostly to describe communitarian movements, and they stand in opposition to most residentially defined communities, whose members live in proximity due principally to economic organization. Much of the opposition to private schooling has been based precisely upon the exclusionary and separatist consequences of such closure. The cases described earlier, ranging from the German communities in the United States to the Turkish communities in Germany, illustrate this opposition.

The ideology of the common public school in the United States has been based on the premise that a school serving a residentially defined community provides a much more democratic and socially integrating form of integenerational closure—bringing together children of different religions, different social classes, and different ethnic groups and thereby bringing their families closer together—than does a school serving an intentional community, whether ethnic, religious, or social-elitist. In general, this premise has been well grounded; but in recent years, the residential area has ceased to be a functional community among adults except in unusual instances like Tucker County, or like Hyde Park where most adults work in the neighborhood where they live.

At its worst, the separatist and exclusionary tendency of a tightly knit community imposes costs on the children of the community. They are not emancipated from the parochialism of their parents; they are not confronted with differing values and the freshness of view such differences can bring. They may be unequipped to enter the heterogeneity and disorder of the larger society and thus either confined to the narrow frame within which they grew up or forced to suffer a serious culture shock when they leave their protected habitat.

FUNCTIONAL COMMUNITIES AND EQUALITY OF OPPORTUNITY

A question that has not been raised is the impact of functional communities of the sort I have described on the level of opportunity for children from differing social backgrounds.

There are several kinds of effects. One fundamental issue, which arises with respect to children in an extremely close community such as a religious commune, is the issue of just how children are deprived or benefited by the constraints-cum-attention imposed by the family and community. The constraints imposed by some religious communities sometimes extend to a refusal to allow the children of the community to attend high school outside the community with noncommunity children. The issue is not really an empirical one, for to decide empirically "what is best for the child" requires knowing what the child's future might be. If the child will leave the community, it is clear that some prior exposure to the broader world will be beneficial. But that very exposure may well determine whether the child leaves the community. And if the child leaves, it has a much broader range of opportunities, together with many outcomes far more miserable, than if it stays and becomes a respected and active adult member of the community.

In short, the child loses one kind of opportunity—the opportunity for success in the larger world—by remaining embedded within the narrow constraints of the community and gains another kind—the opportunity to have the warmth, respect, and satisfaction of a member of the community as an adult. It may be that the only satisfactory resolution of the issue lies not in decisions on specific cases but in an allocation of rights vis-à-vis the child between the family, the community, and the state.

This first issue concerning the effect of functional communities on opportunity is one that arises principally with the most fully closed communities: communes and close religious communities like certain Amish groups. A second, however, arises even in relatively weak functional communities.

In a social structure with closure, the feedback that occurs facilitates the development of *reputations*. In a structure without closure, reputations are nonexistent.

A structure with intergenerational closure facilities *inheritance* of reputations. An example from Tucker County illustrates this well. The man (who may be called Joe X) with the back injured from work in the mines and the Mexican-Indian wife had a well-deserved reputation as a ne'er-do-well. He lived with his wife and two children in a two-room shack beside the road, surrounded by broken-down automobiles. His children, of course, went to school. They did not, of course, get much support and encouragement at home. And because of the intergenerational closure of the community, the father's reputation was inherited by the son.

The son, Joe Junior, left school early, got a girl pregnant, and moved with her into a trailer next to his father's old shack. He is something of a hell-raiser and appears headed toward a career of ne'er-do-well. To what extent this outcome is due to the home environment and to what extent the transmitted reputation itself had an impact within the school is difficult to know. But suppose for a moment that Joe X and his wife, although otherwise no different, had been exemplary in the environment they provided for doing homework and fulfilling school requirements. The reputation that descended from Joe to Joe Junior would still have been there and would have been a difficult impediment for Joe Junior to overcome.

This process is true to a lesser extent in Hyde Park, lesser both because the community has less intergenerational closure and because of the antistereotyping values held by most Hyde Parkers. Yet the feedback channels are there, and despite the values, there is some inheritance of reputation—more than in an anomic suburb. As a result, some go through school with an advantage not possessed by others. A child of a distinguished professor inherits a portion of the parent's reputation, a possession that another child lacks.

This transmission of the social structure of one generation to the next in a close community, partly through inheritance of the parent's reputation by the child, has long been noted by sociologists and others. *Elmtown's Youth, Middletown*, and other ethnographic accounts document this inheritance and show its effects. In the absence of a functional community, the prostitute's daughter and the ne'er-do-well's son are no longer hampered by their parents' reputations and have an opportunity hampered only by the direct impact of their parents' activities on their own. Reputations will arise within the school because every school is a functional community of the children within it, but in the absence of intergenerational closure the children's reputations in school are not inherited from the parents.

There is, however, another effect of functional communities on the opportunity of children from different social backgrounds. As the examples above indicate, the inheritance of reputation operates to provide differential opportunity within a community and within a school. But there is an effect that acts to equalize the opportunities of children from different backgrounds in a functional community. The effect can be seen by asking the question: What parents, on average, benefit more from a system with intergenerational closure like that of Figure A, compared to Figure B: educationally and economically advantaged parents or educationally and economically disadvantaged parents?

The general effects of a system with such closure are to provide additional resources for parents in their interactions with school, supervision of their children's behavior, and supervision of their children's associations, both with others their own age and with adults. The feedback that a parent receives from friends and associates, either unsolicited or in response to questions, provides extensive additional resources that aid the parent in monitoring the school and the child. The norms that parents, as part of their everyday activity are able to establish, act as important aids in socializing children.

All parents can well use such resources, but the parents in most desperate need of them are the parents with least personal resources: parents with little education, few organizational skills, little self-confidence, and little money. These are the disadvantaged parents of disadvantaged children. It is these parents and their children who are most severely harmed when the school is not embedded in a functional community with intergenerational closure. There are various social phenomena that reflect this. One of the most prominent is the extreme difference in capacity of bringing up their children as they would like experienced by lower-class parents in rural areas and in the city.

An illustration of the city's lack of the resources provided by intergenerational closure and the extent to which some parents will go to compensate for them is given by an example of a third-grade class in a school in Harlem in New York City. The teacher noticed that in her class of 30 there were some children who at the end of the school day did not tarry to play with the others but immediately left the school grounds and in a determined fashion headed for home. After some time, she identified three children who always showed this pattern after school. As the year wore on, she queried each of the three children in turn. From each independently she got the same story. The child had fifteen minutes to get from school to home and remained inside the apartment for the rest of the day. Each of these mothers had given her children explicit and absolute instructions to be home within that limit. None of the three was allowed to play with other children outside school except under parent's supervision. It was not that the three formed a group and could play together. Their mothers had acted independently, each hitting upon the same strategy to protect her child from the ravages of the city streets.

The point to the illustration should be evident: None of the 30 mothers had a supporting functional community within which norms governing their children's behavior could develop, a community that would aid them in bringing up their children. In its absence, three who did not work and could monitor their children's actions had arrived at a solution: to forbid their children any activity outside the house except for school.

Parents at all social and educational levels need these resources as an aid in raising their children and monitoring their schooling, but it is clear that those parents most seriously deprived by their absence are those with least resources of their own, the most disadvantaged.

To describe the intergenerational closure of functional communities as a "resource" for parents in raising their children is more than a figure of speech. The extraordinary social mobility that children from lower-class backgrounds, both rural and urban, have had in previous generations in America was accomplished by families with meager tangible resources. The parents had little money and little education. Yet their children showed the "middle-class virtues" of hard work, diligence, respect for the teacher, and good behavior in school, qualities that served them well in preparing them for further education and the mobility it brought. Where did the resources come from to develop and nurture this behavior in children that brought them later rewards?

These children were surrounded by functional communities, either in rural areas or in ethnic neighborhoods of urban areas. At this point it is only a conjecture, but it may well be that the critical resource these parents had, which many modern parents do not, were those functional communities, with the norms, sanctions, and rewards that enabled them to shape the lives of the young. If this is so, it enabled lower-class parents to raise children in a middle-class manner. In contrast—if this conjecture is correct—the decline of such communities in the present leaves those parents without a strong set of personal resources—whether middle-class parents or lower-class ones— able only to raise children in a lower-class manner.

VALUE CONSISTENCY

A functional community is neither a necessary nor a sufficient condition for value consistency, though the two have some affinity. Value consistency grows through the interactions that are found in a functional community and when it exists facilitates the norms that grow up in such a community. But there are value cleavages in functional communities that may be intense. For example, in a highly stratified small town some of the families at the lower end of the stratification ladder may actively reject the values dominant in the community.

At the same time, there are collections of people who exhibit value consistency but who constitute no functional community at all. Parents of children attending certain schools of choice, whether in the public or the private sector, often constitute such a collection. In some cities there are elementary schools that exhibit a particular educational philosophy such as open classrooms or basic education and attract parents who agree with that philosophy. Parents and children may even be required to sign a contract specifying the rules they will observe. These parents, and their children, exhibit a high degree of value consistency but are strangers drawn from throughout the city.

At the secondary level, alternative schools attract students on the basis of their own and their parents' values concerning schooling, but they seldom constitute a functional community.

Many private "independent" schools project certain educational philosophies and attract parents who agree with those philosophies. Quaker schools, for example, tend to have a character quite different from the typical preparatory school of the northeast (more nurturant, less competitive, less academically exacting, more environmentally and anti-nuclear activist). Military academies express a value system almost directly opposite and attract parents with these values.

In contrast to these schools, many private schools organized along religious lines not only have value consistency but also constitute a functional community. Families attend the same religious services and know one another. Thus, private schools differ considerably in this regard: nearly all have a high degree of value consistency, but not all are part of a functional community.

I will use the term *value community* to describe a collection of people who share similar values about education and child rearing but who are not a functional community. As the examples above indicate, some public schools of choice and some private schools in the independent sector have students whose parents are members of a value community but not of a functional community.

Despite these differences among current schools, there are important differences between the value communities that exist now and those that existed in the past and were generated by the functional communities of the past.

When residential areas served by a school were functional communities, it was not true that all members of the community shared the same values. Remaining traces of those communities suggest how the value differences were generated. In Tucker County, West Virginia, the man who brings up his children in a shack along the road surrounded by broken-down automobiles does not share all the values of the farm family down the road whose children have their homework done every day and never miss a day of school or of Sunday school. The difference in values may be in part brought about by Joe X's rejection of a set of values that place him low in the status hierarchy; or it may be that the value differences were what led him in the first place to adopt a style of life that puts him low in the status hierarchy. Whatever the origin of the differences, it is always perfectly clear which values are dominant. There is a clear and consistent set of norms in the community, which express these dominant values; and the degree of conformity to these norms determines, with few exceptions, the position of individuals and families in the status hierarchy. People conform differentially to these norms, in some cases because the status rewards, always in short supply, are not sufficient to balance the pleasures of deviant actions. This differential conformity brings differential status.

The end result is that whatever diversity of values exists in a functional community, one set of values is dominant, and others that differ from them are privately held or narrowly shared but are clearly dominated in the school and community by those from which they deviate. In fact, in some such communities most people will be behaving according to a set of values—the dominant set—that they themselves do not hold privately. Or we may even say that many people accept a set of values that they did not choose and with which, privately, they do not agree.

Two major changes have occurred to change this state of affairs. First, the daily activities of persons who live in proximity are much less often with one another, much more often with others outside, so persons in proximity are not required by the exigencies of life to come to terms with one another. This loss of inward-directed activities constitutes the decline of the residentially based functional community. Second, there has been a communications invasion from the outside, in the form of mass media. Thus, the communications and attention that were in the past directed toward others within the residential community have not merely been redirected to other persons outside that community; they have been redirected toward the mass media in various forms. These new sources of communication, unconstrained by the norms that once dominated the community, now offer values that deviate sharply from those and provide a base of legitimation for the deviant values. No longer is there uncontested dominance of a set of values; different values can exist simultaneously, until some event creates a conflict. It is this change that has made the task of a principal of a public school with attendance based on residence a difficult and sometimes intolerable one. In schools that were based on functional communities, the task of the principal in maintaining and exercising authority in a school was first to discover the dominant set of values in the community, and the norms supporting those values, and then to exercise authority accordingly, imposing sanctions to enforce the norms.[1]

[1]Because the dominance of a set of values carried with it a status hierarchy, as described above, this meant that the principal would be under some inducement to observe the status hierarchy, behaving differently to persons according to their position in this hierarchy. Such differential treatment on the part of the principal and school staff was an important source of inequality

A principal of a school of today in which attendance is based on residence has no set of dominant community values to uphold. Instead, there are a number of contending values, each claiming legitimacy, and at least some of them capable of being backed up by legal suits in court. It was once very unusual for a principal or superintendent to be engaged in legal battles. Now it is commonplace.

A principal with strong personal force can bring it about that a particular set of values becomes dominant within the school. But the potential for challenge to such values is always there, whether from parents who support their son in his refusal to obey a dress code, from a teacher's union that backs up a teacher's grievance about extracurricular burdens, from a parent who objects to prayer in the school, or from a parent who objects to the absence of prayer in the school. The principal no longer has the strength of a tightly knit functional community to support policies and administrative actions and may easily be defeated by such a challenge, with authority undermined from that time forward.

The absence of a value consensus based on a functional community has led with increasing frequency to the creation of schools based on value communities that have no functional community base. In the public sector, this is exemplified by schools, both at the elementary and secondary levels, in which attendance is based not on residence but on choice of school by parent and child. These schools may differ in educational philosophy or in curricular emphasis, but their distinguishing property is that children attend them by their own and their parents' choice and in so doing agree to accept the set of values around which the school is organized.

---

of opportunity in such communities. It was especially inequitous when the status hierarchy as carried over by family from the past did not correspond to actual behavior and those high in the hierarchy failed to conform to norms without sanctions. The popular country song "Harper Valley PTA," narrated by the town's divorcée mother of a junior high school daughter, illustrates this well. But the Harper Valleys in modern society are largely a thing of the past.

In the private sector, many schools are based on value communities that have little grounding in functional communities. Schools in the independent sector ordinarily have a small core of families who know each other well, share a set of values, and are perhaps a residue of one or another social elite in the city (or other area where the school is located). Around this is a much larger population of families who have little social connection to one another or to the core and who enroll their children in school either because of agreement with the values of this core group or because of agreement with the values of the school (which may, of course, coincide with the core group's values). These schools can hardly be said to constitute a functional community of adults, and the children in them may be drawn away from the functional communities of children who attend the neighborhood public school. Nevertheless, they constitute a homogeneous value community.

Catholic schools attended primarily by non-Catholic black students, which is common in large central cities, can be described in much the same way as this. There is often a core of Catholic students, who attend the same parish church and know each other, and a large periphery of non-Catholics, many of whose parents do not know each other. These schools perform, for inner-city black families, the same kind of function that the independent schools do for upper-middle-class families.

Religiously sponsored schools which have student bodies that share that religion (most Catholic schools, conservative and evangelical Christian schools, Lutheran schools, Jewish schools, and others) constitute first of all strong value communities, with the religious values at least as dominant as the community values were in the schools of the past based on geographic communities, but they also are in most cases based on a functional community that shares the same place of worship. These are different from the geographically based functional communities of the past because they are based on interaction in only one arena of life, religion. For that reason they may escape some of the faults of schools based on largely closed geographically based functional communities described earlier (such as the transmission of the community's status system across generations), while retaining the capacity to maintain and reinforce a set of values. It is probably also true that the values they maintain are less easily manipulated to serve the interests of dominant families than were those of the geographically based functional communities that have largely vanished.

As evident in the discussion above, the consequences of a value community in the school are great. Such a school is easy to manage and easy to teach in. The balance of power lies not with the children but with the teachers and the principal. Such a school may be oppressive to some of its students because of the consistency of values. If its clientele are there by choice, however, it is less likely to be oppressive than a traditional value community based on a geographic functional community; and it is not a school that suffers from disorder and absence of structure.

CONCLUSION

The preceding sections have described a set of social changes that have extensive implications for the way children grow up and for the way schools function. These in turn have extensive implications for the kinds of questions we ask about schools and the way we look for answers. It implies that we look at schools not merely as places where individual children learn, or fail to learn, but as social organizations with particular structures and with particular links to the communities in which they are found. As social organizations with an internal structure and an environment, they make improbable the kind of connection between "inputs" and "outputs" that forms the basis for the way we often think about schools and the way we carry out research on them. Rather, the organizations that we call schools contain many members with different interests, sometimes in conflict, and it is out of the interaction of those interests in a particular structure that changes come about in the young persons who constitute the largest portion of their inhabitants. Another way of putting it is that schools are not merely passive containers of resources that add up to produce some effect. They consist of active persons pursuing goals under constraints of the internal organizational structure and the environment.

Research should inform the way we think about schools and the policies we initiate to improve their value for children. Yet research that appropriately examines this interaction of interests of the different actors who make up schools and their environments and the structures within which the interaction occurs cannot yet be carried out in a systematic way; it exists only in rare perceptive ethnographic accounts of what goes on in schools. But because the changes that occur in children and youth as a result of schooling are only a residue of these day-to-day activities, the ethnographic accounts cannot capture the differential residues left by different combinations of resources, structures, and interests in different schools. It remains for systematic research to document those differential residues as well as to provide some indication of what it is about the combination that brings about these differences.

If systematic research is to accomplish this, it must capture, better than it ordinarily does, indicators of those aspects of the organization and its environment that are most important in bringing about changes in children and young persons. It must also examine not merely the narrow change in cognitive skills but a broader range of changes that schools help bring about. Finally, because schools not only bring about changes in the young but are also resources for families, the research must examine how different kinds of schools affect the parents' capability of carrying out their task of raising children.

In short, the systematic or quantitative research implied by the perspective I have taken here must be based on a far richer view of the social processes that make up a school than has been characteristic of "input–output" studies of school effects. There is no implication that systematic quantitative research should give way to more ethnographic accounts of what goes on in a particular school, for such accounts fail to provide good evidence on what the effects of these social processes are. Rather, the implication is that quantitative research—which is fully satisfactory for measuring the residues of these processes (i.e., what we ordinarily think of as effects of schools)—must be sufficiently informed about the character of social processes within the school, and between the school and the surrounding community, that appropriate measures of these processes are obtained. In this way, and with research designs that involve extensive comparison between schools, the next level of understanding of how schools affect the children and youth who inhabit them can be attained.

CHAPTER 9

Moral Education and School Social Organization

CHARLES E. BIDWELL

For some time, the sociology of schools has been dominated by a definition of the school as an array of resource stocks—such things, for example, as teachers, specialist staff, books, subject matter content, and time. For this definition, we owe something to the economists (e.g., Murnane, 1975; Thomas, 1977) and psychologists (e.g., Carroll, 1963; Wiley, 1976). However, it has been widely used and elaborated in studies of educational status attainment, especially studies that relate attainment to social stratification (e.g., Alexander, Cook, and McDill, 1978; Alexander and McDill, 1976; Hauser, 1971; Hauser, Sewell, and Alwin, 1976; Heyns, 1974; Kerckhoff, 1974; Rosenbaum, 1976; Sewell, Haller, and Portes, 1969).

Studies of social organizational effects on school learning that define schools as resource stocks treat such learning as an outcome of biases in the distribution of resources among a school's students. The social organization of schooling itself thereby remains unanalyzed. In contrast, for example, to

Charles E. Bidwell • Departments of Education and Sociology, University of Chicago, Chicago, IL 60637.

Durkheim (1961) or Waller (1961), the resource analysts have not paid much attention to the social structure of the school, even though this structure organizes not only the way schooling resources are distributed but also the way they are combined to affect what students learn. Thus, it should not surprise us that the resource-centered approach has yielded rather modest returns.

Now, however, certain of our colleagues—especially Barr and Dreeben (1977, 1983) and Sørensen and Hallinan (1977) have brought schooling processes more directly into social organizational theories of school learning. Moreover, various empirical studies that have incorporated explicit schooling process variables have demonstrated palpable effects of such processes on what students learn (e.g., Barr and Dreeben, 1983; Coleman, Hoffer, and Kilgore, 1982; Heyns, 1978; Rutter, Maughan, Mortimore, and Ouston, 1979).

Sørensen and Hallinan (1977), for example, in their social organizational model of schooling, attend in part to the resource distribution question (how the social structure of schools may affect students' opportunities to learn), but they go on to ask how these structures also may affect the effort that students expend on school work. This further question substantially broadens the analysis to see school social structure as the locus of an economy of incentives to which students may respond and as a means through which students may acquire academically pertinent motives. Here, however, we see a significant limitation of the new social organizational approach, namely, a rather narrow focus on school learning as academic learning. In practice, this focus becomes even narrower—on school learning as what can be measured by tests of verbal or quantitative achievement.

THE COMMUNAL AND THE MORAL IN EDUCATION

Whatever the bearing of cognitive capacity on social participation, we can surely agree that other human traits are also important, some of them equally so, for such participation.

Many of these traits are at least potentially open to the influence of schooling. Although among this wider array of traits are those that might broadly be thought of as aesthetic and appreciative, my present interest is in moral traits and in the ways in which moral socialization may occur in the course of a student's experience of school. More specifically, I am interested in the ways in which schooling may affect the acquisition and development of values and normative commitments and may affect their organization into motivated patterns of social conduct. My especial interest is in the ways in which schooling may affect capacities for the reflective moral judgment that, one would hope, undergirds both commitment and conduct.

I shall be arguing less for a new conceptualization of the school than for a return to two long-standing and closely related themes in the sociology of education: the school as a community and the school as an agent of moral socialization. In the course of my discussion, I shall try to suggest ways in which the recruitment of students and teachers to schools and the social organization of schools are interrelated and how, in turn, the resulting social forms may affect the school's potency as, on the one hand, an agent of value and norm transmission and, on the other, a setting for the development of the capacity for moral judgment.

I shall proceed from two assumptions: (1) that there is no sharp separation between the cognitive and moral domains in education and (2) that education is more than the sheer transmission of culture. Instead, I think of formal education as comprised of an interrelated constellation of activities through which students form those values, beliefs, emotions, skills, and intellectual habits that may enable them to conduct a life. In this process, whether from the student's or from the teacher's point of view, knowing and valuing, skill and commitment, are complementary and interactive.

A conception of what is worth knowing underlies a school's curriculum, and the curriculum and a teacher's own specification and use of it are matters of critical judgment about aspects of right conduct. They embody a set of commitments to professional standards of content and instructional performance. So, too, from the student's side, the academic content and activities of education are matters of critical moral judgment, and the direction and vigor with which they are pursued are consequences of commitments to standards of conduct (whether they are standards espoused by the school staff, a circle of peers, or some other of the student's points of normative reference).

In sum, decisions about what is to be taught and how it is to be taught entail teachers' moral judgments and commitments. The results of these decisions become objects of moral judgment and decision by students. Moreover, to the extent that students encounter variation in others' moral judgments and commitments about the content and activities of schooling—which variation may occur among and between teachers and fellow students—opportunities for their own practice of moral judgment about a very immediate component of their lives, and the complexity of such judgments, should be heightened. In the course of making these judgments, students gain habits of moral criticism and judgment that will bear at once upon their conduct in school and subsequently on their participation in the society beyond the school.

Durkheim (1961), writing primarily about the early years of schooling, assumed that the school class becomes a powerful agent of moral socialization when its own division of labor and authority structure are constructed to be a microcosm of life in society. Thus, moral education would come about by virtue of the child's habituation to life in the classroom and the later generalization of these habits to life in society.

By contrast, I shall take the position that, past the early childhood years, moral socialization occurs substantially through opportunities for the exercise of moral judgment, the consequent formation of normative commitments, and the realization of these commitments in conduct. The question here is how the social organization of schools may affect the incidence of such opportunities. To pursue this question, I shall restrict my attention to the senior high school (with some passing reference to college).

The idea of the school as community enters because

variation of school social organization toward or away from communal forms should affect the content, frequency, and diversity of students' opportunities for moral judgment. My treatment of community and its application to the study of moral education derives from Max Weber's taxonomic discussion of communal and associative and of open and closed social relationships (Weber, 1947: 87–157).

Weber (1947:136) distinguishes "communal" from "associative" social relationships according to the degree to which they are based on a subjective mutual feeling by the parties to the relationship that they "belong together." Associative relationships, unlike those based on this "we" feeling, take root in "the rationally motivated adjustment of interests or a similarly motivated agreement," although the basis of the adjustment or agreement may just as well be considerations of value as of "expediency."

With respect to communal relationships, Weber is careful to note that common traits (even so primordial a trait as common language) do not in themselves entail communal ties. It is only when common traits foster "the feeling of belonging together," primarily by fostering face-to-face interaction, that common traits result in a communal relationship.

Weber (1947:139) continues by distinguishing open from closed relationships, whether communal or associative, according to the degree to which they can be entered upon by "anyone who wishes to participate and who is actually in a position to do so." Like "we" feeling, openness and closure may be grounded on tradition, affect, or the rationality of either values or expediency.

Weber extends these distinctions from simple pairwise social ties to collectivities, which presumably are to be classified according to the modal tendencies observed among their constituent dyads. Moreover, the distinctions apply to corporate groups (those characterized by formal rules of procedure and administrative direction) just as much as to less formally enacted collectivities (Weber, 1947:145–148). The existence of formal rules and an administration may have some effect on the likelihood of communal and open social relationships in corporate groups, but not an effect of overwhelming power.

Even though schools are characterized by a heavy admixture of associative relationships (not only the contractual bond between school staff and school boards, but also the relationships generated when students, for example, have chosen to attend a specialized high school), the extent to which communal relationships are added to this mixture is evidently highly variable.

Waller (1961) devoted a good deal of attention to the various collective representations that might foster communal relationships in schools (among students and between students and teachers), and Meyer (1970) has proposed that "chartered" schools are especially likely to develop communal characteristics. Meyer's analysis, in fact, implies that as schools tend to become closed corporate groups, the ground is prepared for the emergence of communal ties among their members (student-to-student, student-to-teacher, and, as we shall suggest, teacher-to-teacher as well).

Whether schools are open or closed is among their more salient properties. In current terminology, this property is called *selectivity*. Weber (1947:143) remarks that the "maintenance of quality" and, derivatively, of honor or prestige is a principal reason for closure, and this rationale is fully evident with respect to restricted student enrollment and both collegial and administrative screening of candidates for faculty posts. So, also, are other of Weber's posited bases for closure, such as a rational orientation to value maintenance (e.g., schools sponsored by sectarian religious denominations), or self-interest (e.g., specialized vocational schools), or tradition (e.g., many private boarding schools).

MORAL TRANSMISSION AND MORAL JUDGMENT

From these Weberian ideas about closure and communalism, whether applied to between-school or within-school contrasts, one can proceed to propositions about the effectiveness of schooling either as moral transmission or as a means of developing capacity for moral judgment. First, however, we must define school closure. The greater the number and rigor of recruitment criteria and the more pervasive and substantively consistent their application across the membership, staff, and students alike, the greater the degree of closure that characterizes a school, or any of its subunits (such as a department or debate team).

Next, we shall follow Weber by assuming that social similarity promotes face-to-face interaction. We shall also assume that interpersonal influence is the principal means by which values and normative commitments are formed or changed. It follows that the greater the degree of a school's closure, the stronger and more consistent should be the school's transmission effects on students' value and norm learning and moral commitments.

Here we have the familiar notion of the school as a kind of moral hothouse, in which pervasive, cohesive, and substantively consistent ties among students and between students and teachers cumulate to create a powerful, convergent development of students' beliefs and commitments to rules of conduct. This is the argument that underlies Newcomb's (1943) famous analysis of the "peculiar potency" of Bennington College in its heyday, and it is consistent with the weight of the evidence in the Feldman–Newcomb (1969) synthesis of research on college effects.

I have suggested, however, that there is more to moral education than value or norm transmission and that a fuller conception of the process must embrace means by which capacity for moral reflectiveness and judgment (and for the normative commitments that result from reflective judgment) may be formed. We need not abandon the notion that moral transmission is a part of moral education or with it the centrality of structures of interpersonal influence in moral education, but we must go further.

If the incidence of mechanisms of moral transmission and the distribution of opportunities for moral reflection and judgment are strong functions of the occurrence of closure and hence of communal social ties in a school, the question opens how the distribution of closure and ties may affect the incidence of moral consensus among a school's members and consequently affect students' opportunities to receive moral messages or exercise moral judgment.

We can begin by allowing for variation in schools' curricular and social structural differentiation and for variation in the situation of the individual student with respect to this differentiation. Weber (1947:142) notes that closure may vary within groups—for example, reliance within guilds or castes on competition or on entitlement as mechanisms for allocating access to the group's resources and benefits. With respect to schools, curricular or social structural differentiation may vary in conjunction with variation in the closure of curricular or social structural subunits. Depending on the form and content of curricular and social structural differentiation and the degree to which the student's perceived school work is encapsulated within one or another of the parts of the differentiated curricular and social structure, opportunities for moral reflection and judgment and the complexity of the opportunities afforded should vary.

Consider first a school faculty. With minor exceptions like peer tutoring, faculties are closed against students, but in other respects their closure varies substantially. So far as the closure of entire faculties is concerned, the history of the teaching occupation is in part a history of increasing closure as states have established licensure and have tended to elaborate the criteria by which prospective teachers become licensed to teach.

However, in the United States and to a very substantial degree elsewhere these criteria remain sparse and relaxed. So far as governmental regulation is concerned, school teaching is a comparatively open occupation. Degrees of closure are mainly a matter of additional criteria imposed by individual schools or local authorities. In many public schools in the United States, the closure of the teaching ranks is largely a question of minimizing salary costs, so that closure varies with teacher supply. By way of example, take the current reduction in the closure of mathematics and science teaching, in which a scarcity of certified teachers is dealt with not by raising inducements for the certified but by relaxing enforcement of certification requirements. Nevertheless, among certain public schools and many private schools in this country use of closure to maintain quality and prestige and either traditional criteria or a rational orientation to value maintenance (e.g., parochial or alternative schools) may lead to the imposition of further recruitment criteria, such as advanced degrees, occupational experience, intelligence, or religious affiliation.

Within a high-school faculty, one can see substantial variation in the use of such subdivisions as subject matter or such broader curricular divisions as the academic, general, and vocational programs to define points of closure. When the subject matter specialization of teachers is used to maintain school quality or prestige, it defines a faculty that is closed not only externally but at various internal boundaries as well. Although academic speciality may be the most frequent basis for the formation of closed faculty subgroups, other bases also may be observed, although often in conjunction with subject matter specialty (e.g., in a religiously sponsored high school, orthodox belief as a stronger criterion for membership in humanities or social science than in science or mathematics subfaculties).

From our assumptions about the relationship between closure, social similarity, and moral consensus it follows that the boundaries that define areas of closure of or within a school's faculty are also likely to define areas of cohesion and consensus, the latter with a content that corresponds to the grounding of closure—for example, belief in the sanctity of learning, in the ascendancy of a subject matter, in the faith of a born-again Christian, in the legitimacy of political activism, or in scientific skepticism.

If this argument is right, then to the degree that a school faculty itself is closed (the greater the number and rigor of entrance criteria) and the less internally differentiated it is with respect to closure, the more potent it should be as an agent of moral transmission. However, to the degree that the faculty is divided into closed subgroups, the less potent this agency should be. Moreover, when the criteria of subgroup closure define lines of moral difference, the way is prepared for either transmission effects on subgroups of students who are exposed primarily or exclusively to a given faculty subgroup or for the exposure to the moral differences, contrasts, and tensions that I believe fosters the development of capacity for moral judgment.

The probability of each of these outcomes should be a function, in turn, of the incidence of closed relationships within the school's student body. When an entire student body is relatively closed (as in a highly selective academic or otherwise specialized high school), cohesion and moral consensus should be widespread among students.

If the school's faculty also is closed, but the criteria of closure for students and faculty produce disparate beliefs or norms as between faculty and students (e.g., a prestige-seeking school that recruits highly qualified faculty and students from wealthy but Philistine families), the stage is set for an intensification of the faculty–student warfare so graphically described by Waller (1961), for a concomitant intensification of student solidarity, and for powerful moral transmission effects confined within the student ranks. If, as may be more likely, there is a good deal of moral consistency between the criteria of faculty and student recruitment (e.g., a religious school or the Bronx High School of Science), transmission effects again are favored, but with an exceptional strength that results from the mutual reinforcement of faculty and peer influence. Such reinforcement presumably underlay the peculiar potency of Bennington College.

Consider next the possibility that closure within a student body may vary in pervasiveness and intensity. Setting aside for present purposes the formation of informal student circles and cliques, the main lines of such variation in a high school are probably to be found in the curriculum and the extracurriculum.

Curricular Differentiation

Sørensen (1970) has described a number of ways in which curricular tracks may be more or less closed. As examples of this variation, think of schools with academically self-contained tracks to which students are assigned early and from which they have few chances to exit; schools with tracks that are academically self-contained but that have multiple entry and exit points; schools that track students on an independent basis subject by subject; and schools that track students late after a substantial basis of common course work.

If, as seems likely, closed faculty relationships are specialty-based, then as the pervasiveness and the intensity of student track closure decline, the likelihood that students will be exposed to a diversity of faculty values and normative commitments should increase, becoming more diverse as the number and cohesiveness of closed faculty subgroups grow. Given the likely moral heterogeneity and low aggregate cohesion of an internally open student body, as exposure to a morally diverse faculty increases, the likelihood of peer transmission effects should decline.

To sum up this part of the argument, curricular differentiation should provide a prime basis for the closure of faculty subgroups. Especially when curricular specialization is reinforced by additional faculty recruitment criteria, this subgroup structure should provide the conditions of strong faculty-to-student transmission effects, but only when a school's student body forms closed subgroups that are isomorphic with those found in the faculty. The strength of such effects should arise from reinforcing effects of instruction, student–teacher ties, and ties among students.

As the student body becomes more open internally, the probability and strength of transmission effects should decline, and opportunities for the formation of judgmental capacity should increase, in rough proportion to the pervasiveness and intensity of closure among curricularly bounded faculty subgroups and the pervasiveness and intensity of their moral differentiation. In these circumstances, then, the faculty, the curriculum, and instructional activities, insofar as they become agents of moral education, should provide students with opportunities for moral reflection and judgment.

Extracurricular Differentiation

The extracurriculum presents matters of further interest. By virtue of self-selection, we might expect the members of various extracurricular organizations to differ in their values or normative commitments (e.g., members of varsity teams versus newspaper staffers versus members of rock or stamp clubs). Even though extracurricular organizations (with the exception of those that require certain specific skills) may be formally open, they often develop *de facto* closure based in part on the self-selection of members and in part on the formation of peer networks around nodes of extracurricular participation. Therefore, in most high schools we might expect extracurricular organizations to function mainly as agents of moral transmission.

However, Barker and Gump (1964) argued for a threshold effect of school enrollment on high-school students' participation in the extracurriculum. They asserted that in small schools the tendency for any high school to preserve some minimal array of extracurricular activities would open a range of extracurricular opportunities to every student and, indeed, impel faculty to induce students to try their hands at a variety of after-school activities. If Barker and Gump are correct, below some threshold of enrollment we might expect the extracurriculum to have positive effects on students' capacities for moral judgment because small enrollments allow students to take part in activities of diverse value and normative provenance.

CONCLUSIONS

In the foregoing pages, I have tried to do three things. First, I have sought to bring schooling outcomes in addition to academic attainment back into view. Although I have discussed moral education, it should be of some interest to sociologists of the school to broaden the array of outcome variables still further. Second, I have argued that moral education involves not only the transmission of values and normative orientations but also the formation of capacity for reflective moral judgment. Third, I have presented a Weberian argument in which the criteria of faculty and student recruitment and allocation jointly provide social organizational conditions under which schools may be more or less effective in moral transmission or in the formation of capacity for moral judgment. These also are conditions under which the principal sources of such effectiveness are to be found in the faculty, the student body, or in a complementarity of faculty and student influence.

Closing, I should stress that the variables that I think underlie the social organizational means of either moral transmission or judgment formation in schools are for the most part quite open to school policy. At the same time, I should note that if my social organizational argument is correct, efforts to foster moral education by expanding the domain of communal relationships in a school may have various unanticipated outcomes. Whatever the costs of at least certain kinds of curricular differentiation, their possible educative benefits—moral as well as cognitive—should not be ignored.

REFERENCES

Alexander, Karl L. and Edward L. McDill. 1976. "Selection and allocation within schools: some causes and consequences of curriculum placement." *American Sociological Review* 41:963–80.

Alexander, Karl L., Martha Cook, and Edward L. McDill. 1978. "Curriculum tracking and educational stratification: some further evidence." *American Sociological Review* 43:47–66.

Barker, Roger and Paul Gump. 1964. *Big School, Small School*. Stanford, CA: Stanford University Press.

Barr, Rebecca and Robert Dreeben. 1977. "Instruction in classrooms." *Review of Research in Education* 5:89–161.

Barr, Rebecca and Robert Dreeben. 1983. *How Schools Work*. Chicago: University of Chicago Press.

Carroll, John B. 1963. "A model of school learning." *Teachers College Record* 64:723–33.

Coleman, James S., Thomas Hoffer, and Sally Kilgore. 1982. *High School Achievement*. New York: Basic Books.

Durkheim, Emile. 1961. *Moral Education*. Glencoe, IL: Free Press.

Feldman, Kenneth and Theodore M. Newcomb. 1969. *The Impact of College on Students*. San Francisco: Jossey-Bass.

Hauser, Robert M. 1971. *Socioeconomic Background and Educational Performance*. Washington, D.C.: American Sociological Association.

Hauser, Robert M., William H. Sewell and Duane Alwin. 1976. "High school effects on achievement." In William H. Sewell, Robert M. Hauser, and David L. Featherman (eds.), *Schooling and Achievement in American Society*. New York: Academic Press.

Heyns, Barbara. 1974. "Social selection and stratification within schools." *American Journal of Sociology* 79:1434–51.

Heyns, Barbara. 1978. *Summer Learning and the Effects of Schooling*. New York: Academic Press.

Kerckhoff, Alan C. 1974. *Ambition and Attainment: A Study of Four Samples of American Boys*. Washington, D.C.: American Sociological Association.

Meyer, John. 1970. "The charter: conditions of diffuse socialization in schools." Pp. 564–578 in W. Richard Scott (ed.), *Social Processes and Social Structures*. New York: Holt, Rinehart, and Winston.

Murnane, Richard J. 1975. *The Impact of School Resources on the Learning of Inner City Children*. Cambridge, MA: Ballinger.

Newcomb, Theodore M. 1943. *Personality and Social Change*. New York: Dryden Press.

Rosenbaum, James E. 1976. *Making Inequality: The Hidden Curriculum of High School Tracking*. New York: Wiley.

Rutter, Michael, Barbara Maughan, Peter Mortimore, and Janet Ouston. 1979. *Fifteen Thousand Hours*. Cambridge, MA: Harvard University Press.

Sewell, William H., Archibald O. Haller, and Alejandro Portes. 1969. "The educational and early occupational attainment process." *American Sociological Review* 34:82–91.

Sørensen, Aage. 1970. "Organizational differentiation of students and educational opportunity." *Sociology of Education*, 43:355–376.

Sørensen, Aage, and Maureen Hallinan. 1977. "A reconceptualization of school effects." *Sociology of Education*, 50:273–289.

Thomas, J. Alan. 1977. *Resource Allocation in Classrooms*. Final Report to the National Institute of Education (grant no. 4-0794). Chicago: Department of Education, University of Chicago.

Waller, Willard. 1961. *The Sociology of Teaching*. New York: Russell and Russell.

Weber, Max. 1947. *The Theory of Social and Economic Organization*. Glencoe, IL: The Free Press.

Wiley, David E. 1976. "Another hour, another day: quantity of schooling, a potent path for policy." In William H. Sewell, Robert M. Hauser, and David L. Featherman (eds.), *Schooling and Achievement in American Society*. New York: Academic Press.

Author Index

Subject Index